Patrick Howarth is the author of numerous works of history, biography and criticism, including *The Year is 1851* and *George VI*. Eight programmes of his poetry have been broadcast by BBC Radio 3. A former diplomat, serving in Special Operations, he has broadcast for the BBC in five languages. He lives in Sherborne.

Praise for *Atilla: King of the Huns*

'Patrick Howarth, a former diplomat who served in Special Operations, and an intelligent writer of popular history . . . presents Attila as a world statesman who understood the importance of plunder for the Hun balance of payments, and came close to conquering the known world.'

Philip Howard, *The Times*

'. . . Patrick Howarth has just written an enthralling and entirely accessible biography of one of the most maligned and least understood figures in history – Attila, King of the Huns . . . with the aid of some remarkable archaeological finds, Patrick Howarth is able to reassess the character and achievements of Attila and the Hun culture. The truth is far richer and far more impressive than the myth.'

Sherborne Messenger

ATTILA
KING OF THE HUNS
The Man and the Myth

PATRICK HOWARTH

CARROLL & GRAF PUBLISHERS
New York

Carroll & Graf Publishers, Inc.
An imprint of Avalon Publishing Group, Inc.
161 William Street
New York
NY 10038–2607
www.carrollandgraf.com

Attila, King of the Huns first published in the UK by
Constable and Company Ltd 1994
This paperback edition published in the UK by Robinson,
an imprint of Constable & Robinson Ltd 2001

First Carroll & Graf edition 2001

ISBN 0–7867–0930–8

Printed and bound in the EU

To Douglas Blyth

CONTENTS

CONTENTS

ACKNOWLEDGEMENTS

I am deeply grateful to the Hélène Heroys Literary Foundation for its help in enabling me to write this book. I wish too to express my warm thanks to Douglas Blyth and Mark le Fanu.

I owe a deep debt to many people in Hungary, distinguished scholars and others, who gave me so much of their valuable time. Among those I feel I must single out are Colonel László Korsos, Director of the Hungarian Military Museum in Budapest, Dr Ottó Trogmayer, Director of the Ferenc Mora Museum in Szeged, Dr Sándor Bökönyi of Budapest University, Dr Attila Kiss of the Hungarian National Museum in Budapest, and Dr László Gazda and György Mody of the Déri Museum in Debrecen.

I also wish to express special thanks to the Rector of Szeged University, Professor János Csirik, and the Hungarian Academy of Science for the special facilities they afforded me.

Many others have given me freely of their time and to them, listing their names alphabetically, I also want to express my thanks. They include Csanád Bálint, Jocelyne Barthol, Claudine Belayche, Dr Benedict Benedickx, Dr Böhringer, Maté Botos, Father Leonard E. Boyle, H. Charnier, Vanessa Corrick, Miklós Czenthe, Dr Ernst Englisch, Dr István Fodor, J. Freeman, Dr Ferenc Horvath, C. Marion, Anne Monginoux, Dr Margit Nagy, Robert Neiss, Jean-Pierre Ravaux, Lucie Roux, Péter Tomka and Gabriella Vörös.

I could not have written this book without the continual help of my wife Eva, who has the inestimable advantage, for the purposes of this book, of speaking Hungarian as her mother tongue.

ILLUSTRATIONS

CONTEMPORARY RULERS

WESTERN ROMAN EMPIRE

Valentinian II 373–392
Theodosius I 392–395 (see Eastern Empire)
Eugenius 392–394
Honorius 394–423
John 423–425
Galla Placidia (Regent) 425–437
Valentinian III 425–455
Petronius Maximus 455
Avitus 455–456
Majorianus 457–461
Libius Severus 461–465
Anthemius 465–472

EASTERN ROMAN EMPIRE

Valens 364–378
Theodosius I 379–395
Arcadius 395–408
Theodosius II 408–450
Marcian 450–457
Leo I 457–474

HUNS

Mundzuk *c.* 415–420
Ruga 420–434
Bleda 434–445
Attila 445–453
Ellak 453–455

VISIGOTHS

Alaric 391–410
Athaulf 410–415
Sigeric 415
Wallia 415–418
Theodoric 418–451
Thorismund 451–453
Theodoric II 453–466

CHAPTER 1

A MUCH-MALIGNED PEOPLE

In the fifth century AD the Huns, one of the most maligned and least understood of all peoples, established their headquarters – they could hardly be said to have had a capital – near the middle reaches of the river Tisza. The Tisza flows from north to south through Hungary roughly parallel to, and to the east of, the Danube. As it passes through Szeged, Hungary's second city, it is a wide and impressive river.

The countryside here is flat. If you travel from Budapest to Szeged you will not see a hill of any size, and one part of the plain of south-eastern Hungary retains some of the characteristics it had when the Huns occupied it. This is the Hortobagy, where horses abound; there are sheep with twisted horns and there is even a herd of buffaloes. There are curlews and larks, bustards and harriers, and white storks are plentiful. But the predominant impression given by this strange land is of emptiness, a feeling of nothing.

From this plain the Huns in the fifth century controlled, largely through associate or subject peoples, an empire stretching from the Urals to the Rhone. Yet the name of only one of this remarkable people is known, outside Hungary, to anybody except a few specialist historians. The exception is Attila, whose name has been familiar to the masses for fifteen hundred years.

Attila ruled his Hun kingdom for only eight years. But in that time his military prowess was such that he threatened the destruction of the Roman empires in both east and west. At one moment he was at the walls of Constantinople in a position to demand huge tributes in gold. Later he was to be found leading a cosmopolitan army as far west as

Orléans. The year after he was advancing towards Rome, capturing one prosperous Italian city after another.

To his Christian enemies he was known as the Scourge of God, yet the sister of a Roman empress sent him her ring as a way of proposing marriage.

Posterity has for the most part pictured Attila as a bloodthirsty tyrant, yet there is on record a first-hand account of his appearance, his lifestyle and his manner of conducting public business by a distinguished writer, who had the opportunity of observing him at close quarters.[1] From this he emerges as a much more attractive character than his popular reputation would suggest. Of his calibre as a ruler the writer had no doubts. Attila, he declared, 'was a man born to shake the races of the world. The proud man's power was to be seen in the very movements of his body.'

In retrospect the mid fifth century seems to abound in colourful figures: the Empress Galla Placidia, whose tomb is today one of the glories of Ravenna, at one time married to a Visigoth king, at another dragged through the streets as a captive, later effectively ruling the Western Empire; Pope Leo the Great, overcoming by personality and persuasion the dangers of heresy and schism and confronting Attila in an eventful encounter; the Emperor Theodosius II in Constantinople – humane, learned, delighting in theological debate yet continually distracted by the business of war; his principal adviser, the arch-intriguer and eunuch Chrysaphius; his sister, the pious Pulcheria, persuading her own sisters to dedicate themselves to perpetual virginity.

There was St Jerome, retiring to the desert, inducing high-born Roman matrons to accept a similar life of asceticism, railing against the iniquities of the Huns and the Vandals. There were Goth and Vandal rulers defying Rome, even capturing the city and creating their own kingdoms within the long-established boundaries of the Roman Empire.

Towards none of his contemporaries did Attila conduct himself as less than an equal. As a conqueror he towered above them all.

For some fifteen hundred years the Western world has gained its knowledge of the Huns from prejudiced and predominantly hostile sources. The earliest commentators were citizens of the Roman Empire, writing in Latin or Greek, who held the prevailing derogatory view of barbarians. They were succeeded by Christian chroniclers, who condemned the Huns as pagans and regarded Attila as an instrument sent by God to punish people for their sins.

Recently new sources of knowledge have been opened up, principally in the form of archaeological finds. Scientists have extended their fields of study far beyond the empire once controlled by Attila. Hungarians, in particular, have discovered Hun graves along the silk road to China, penetrating, in their studies, deep into the territory of the former Soviet Union. In the West, French archaeologists, among others, have been no less assiduous, finding traces of Hun culture in North Africa and even in England.

The findings have been studied by experts in animal husbandry, military historians and others, and as a result a new understanding of Hun culture has become possible. With it has come an opportunity to reassess the character and achievements of Attila. Should he perhaps be regarded primarily as a ruler who, with a sound appreciation of the importance of plunder – particularly gold – to the Hun economy, exploited to the full the opportunities circumstances afforded him?

Alternatively, was he one of those military commanders who arise from time to time and who, having a vision of conquering most of the known world, are inspired by their vision to advance far towards their goal?

It is possible that he was both.

CHAPTER 2

THE HUNS MOVE WEST

The Huns came westward to Europe from the borders of China. Chinese documents of the Han period refer to a warlike people known as the Hsiung-nu, who may possibly be identified with the Huns. Certainly these people caused Chinese rulers considerable trouble. One of the battles they won was for a time decisive, and they were able as a result to exact valuable tribute in the form of gold, silk and female slaves. In the majestic words of Edward Gibbon, 'a select band of the fairest maidens of China was annually devoted to the rude embraces of the Huns.'[1]

The Great Wall of China was built as a defence against such marauders, but a more effective form of resistance may have been the adoption of some of their methods of mobile warfare. As a result the Hsiung-nu were heavily defeated in a battle early in the first century BC, after which their name seems to have disappeared from Chinese records.[2]

Whether or not the Hsiung-nu were their ancestors, the Huns, even after establishing themselves in central Europe, maintained certain links with China once the Emperor Wu-ti had opened the western silk road.[3] The common practice was for groups of between six and ten families to travel together, each of these social units having its own area for feeding its animals.

From time to time the units would amalgamate with others to form a kind of social cooperative. From within such a cooperative a strong ruler might emerge who would steadily increase his following. He might even become powerful enough to establish a nomadic kingdom and found a dynasty, but the dynasty would survive only so long as it provided strong rulers.[4]

Nomadic kings would lead their peoples into battle in order to increase their resources by plunder, and in this way large areas of territory could be traversed. But such movements might be in any direction. The persistent westward movement of the Huns had other causes, the chief of which was climatic.

In the early centuries of the Christian era there was a widespread movement of peoples. A principal cause of this was a general lowering of temperature in northern Europe. Another, also in northern Europe, was a steady encroachment of land by the sea.

In the steppe lands in the extreme east of Europe cycles of greater or less aridity lasting several hundred years follow each other. About the same time as the temperature fell persistently in northern Europe an exceptionally dry cycle seems to have driven the steppe nomads, Huns among them, westward in search of fodder.[5]

As they advanced westwards the Huns drove in front of them large numbers of refugees seeking to escape from Hun conquest. This was a consequence partly of the Huns' superior military skills and partly of the terror that this strange-looking people seem to have induced.

The Huns' preeminence as warriors derived primarily from their mastery of the horse, secondly from their skill as bowmen. The horses themselves, which were about twenty centimetres shorter at the withers than modern hunters, had both speed and endurance and in many respects were superior to those in western Europe. They had excellent hooves and without shoeing could cover long distances everywhere except on mountain terrain. They regularly travelled a hundred kilometres a day. They also had the ability to find fodder even under snow.

A Roman veterinary surgeon, Vegetius Renatus, described their horses in detail. 'The Hunnish horses', he wrote, 'have large heads, curved like hooks, protruding eyes, narrow nostrils, broad jaws, strong and rigid necks. Their manes hang down to their knees, their ribs are big, their backbones curved, and their tails shaggy. They have very strong shinbones and small feet, their hooves being full and broad, and the soft parts hollow. Their whole body is angular with no fat at all on the rump, nor are there any protuberances on the muscles. The stature is rather long than tall. The trunk is vaulted, and the bones are strong, and the leanness of the horses is striking. But one forgets the ugly appearance of these horses as this is set off by their fine qualities: their sober nature, cleverness and their ability to endure any injuries very well.'[6]

Hun children learned to ride almost as soon as they learned to walk. Outside observers frequently commented on the extraordinary affinity between Hun riders and their horses. The Huns were said to sleep on their horses, to perform their natural functions on them, and even to conduct important business of state on horseback. The fifth-century historian and bishop Count Zosimus may have been exaggerating when he wrote that the Huns were so used to riding that they were sometimes unsteady on their feet when walking.[7] Other commentators wrote of Hun riders and horses being nailed or soldered together. One even stated that 'not even the centaurs grew closer to their horses than they did.'[8]

Hun warriors made a practice of travelling with a number of reserve horses to ensure that they always had a fresh one when needed. Every horse belonging to a particular rider had to resemble as closely as possible the others in his string. The leading Hungarian authority on Hun animals, Professor S. Bökönyi, found in the grave of a Hun warrior the skeletons of two horses and, on measuring them, observed that their sizes were in all respects almost identical.

Professor Bökönyi is also of the opinion that the Huns invented the stirrup.[9] Other historians have given the credit to the Sarmatians.[10] But whatever the truth, there is no doubt that the Huns used stirrups to increase their effectiveness as mounted warriors with devastating effect.

Not the least of the reasons why the Huns inspired so much terror was the speed of their movements. With their system of having reserve horses they could ensure that no messenger travelled faster than they did. As a result the first the occupants of a village or a fort learned of the arrival of a hostile force of Huns was a cloud of dust, followed by the sound of horses' hooves, followed by a rain of arrows.

As bowmen the Huns were no less skilled than they were as horsemen. The bows used by the Romans before they came into contact with mounted warriors, first those of the Persian Empire and later those of the Huns and other eastern peoples, were not very effective weapons. They were only drawn a few centimetres, whereas the Huns developed bows that they could draw twenty or thirty centimetres. A specimen of the so-called reflex bow of the Huns can be seen in the Hungarian Military Museum in Budapest today.

The Huns could fire their arrows up to three hundred metres and could kill a man at half that distance. At fifty metres they could pierce a wild boar, and at thirty metres both bones in the upper thigh of an ox. Tests carried out with a reflex bow on comparable targets have verified these claims.[11]

The Huns' arrows were made of soft wood strengthened with bone inlays, and they had a variety of arrow-heads, some being used for battle, others for hunting. A Hun warrior would normally carry thirty arrows when going into action. These would not last him long, and the supply would be replenished by a kind of mobile ordnance factory consisting of mounted workmen who travelled with the warriors.

A striking force of Hun warriors numbered between five hundred and a thousand men. They began by firing arrows at a distance of about three hundred metres. They would then advance in zig-zag fashion, pretend to withdraw, then advance again. Standing in their stirrups, they could fire their arrows forward, backward or sideways. When early historians wrote of the sky being dark with arrows they were scarcely exaggerating. Surprise and terror were of the essence of Hun tactics. Their whole strategy was, in a number of respects, a forerunner of the twentieth-century blitzkrieg.

The combined effect of climatic changes, the attractions of empire and the blitzkrieg, which was conducted by the Huns over large areas and with conspicuous success, was a mass movement into western Europe, which was probably without precedent. It was not to be repeated on a comparable scale until the late twentieth century, when, suddenly, millions of people from North Africa and, to a lesser extent, from Asia again flooded in. In the earlier migration the main pressure was from the north. In the later it was from the south. In both there was additional pressure from the east.

One instance of a large and fairly homogeneous group of people entering the Roman Empire because of pressure from the Huns occurred three-quarters of the way through the fourth century.

An attack by the Huns on the Ostrogoths led to a mass movement, not only by them, but also by Visigoths towards the Empire's frontier. The Visigoth king, Athanaric, tried to organize a defence of his kingdom, but large numbers of his people, terrified by the prospect of the Huns' approach, petitioned the Emperor Valens in Constantinople to be allowed to settle within the Empire.

Valens, an ill-favoured man physically, has been described variously by latter-day writers as excessively cruel and as well-intentioned. He was evidently lacking in judgement. He made himself temporarily popular by reducing taxation by a quarter, but in the light of the military commitments he entered into it was an ill-considered measure. He was baptized by an Arian bishop and then made himself conspicuous by persecuting the more orthodox Christians.

Valens acceded to the Visigoths' petition, evidently believing that they would provide him with a large force of recruits for his army. But the settlement of the immigrants was badly mishandled. Some were conscripted for frontier duty. Others were sent to the town named, in honour of the Emperor Hadrian, Hadrianople (today Edirne, the frontier town on the Turkish side of the border with Greece). But the great bulk remained where they had arrived and where there was a serious shortage of food.

Seeing the opportunity this presented, a number of the local inhabitants sold the Goths dog-meat and then made a further profit by selling some of the Goths themselves into slavery. Not surprisingly disturbances broke out, which were encouraged by a number of Ostrogoths who had crossed the Danube under two determined leaders, the guardians of their young king.

Fighting continued, in which the Goths achieved some initial success, although they were then driven back. In 378 they returned in greater force, this time being supported by a number of Huns and Alans.

Valens, who had been engaged in a fruitless war against the Persians, returned and was determined to crush all rebellion. For this purpose he was promised support from the Emperor in the west, the talented young Gratian, who was his nephew. Whether from vanity, because he wished to have all the credit for a successful battle, or from a miscalculation of military strengths, Valens decided not to wait for the reinforcements that Gratian offered.

Battle was joined near Hadrianople, and the outcome was a comprehensive victory for the Goths, in which Valens himself and some two-thirds of his army lost their lives. For the first time barbarians who had been allowed to settle inside the Roman Empire had shown themselves capable of defeating a Roman army.

CHAPTER 3

TRIBAL WARFARE

In their travels towards the Roman Empire the Huns were confronted by a variety of peoples, with many of whom they did battle. Some peoples were readier than others to accept the kind of dominion the Huns imposed. Some swelled the flood of refugees. Some provided a valuable accession of manpower to the Hun armies.

The first people whose encounters with the Huns have been described in any detail were the Alans. The territory the Alans occupied at the time of the Huns' approach lay between the rivers Volga and Don and was bounded by the Caucasus mountains.

The Alans have been described as an Iranian people. The grave of one of their chiefs was found to contain his chain-mail of iron, a gold torque, bronze bracelets, a gold-handled sword and some splendid drinking vessels of Persian or central Asian workmanship.[1]

The Roman historian Ammianus Marcellinus wrote of the Alans: 'The Alani extend to the east, near the territories of the Amazons, and are scattered among many populous and wealthy nations, stretching to the parts of Asia which, as I am told, extend up to the Ganges.'

After explaining that they were a nomadic people, who never used the plough and drove their flocks and herds before them, Ammianus went on: 'Nearly all the Alani are men of great stature and beauty; their hair is somewhat yellow, their eyes are terribly fierce; the lightness of their armour renders them rapid in their movements; and they are in every respect equal to the Huns, only more civilized in their food and their manner of life ... As ease is a delightful thing to men of a quiet and placid disposition, so danger and war are a pleasure to the Alani.'

A major battle between the Alans and the Huns was fought in the

370s, which the Huns won conclusively. The Goth historian Jordanes stated that the Huns exhausted the Alans by their incessant attacks, adding that 'by the terror of their features they inspired great fear in those whom perhaps they did not really surpass in war.' However the victory may have been gained, the Alans were the first people occupying substantial territory in Europe to live in large numbers under Hun domination.

Not all Alans accepted this role. Some fled westwards where they would later serve as soldiers both in alliance with and against the Huns. Others moved into the Caucasus, settling in Ossetia, some of whose present inhabitants are certainly their descendants.

The Sarmatians, another people encountered by the Huns in their travels, spoke a language akin to that of the Alans, and were also of Indo-European origin. They expected their young women to take part in warfare, a custom which may have inspired the Greek accounts of a people known as Amazons. The Sarmatians seem to have responded to Hun conquests by adopting the Huns' crossbow, which they learned to shoot backwards. One of the scenes depicted on Trajan's column in Rome is of Sarmatian warriors using their bows in the Hun manner.

That the Sarmatians migrated as far as present-day Hungary, almost certainly driven there by the Huns, is shown by the evidence of their graves.[2] There is also evidence that there were appreciable numbers of Sarmatians fighting in the armies commanded by Attila.

A number of Slav peoples living east of the Vistula were also driven by the Huns towards the Danube. Germanic tribes who came to a greater or lesser degree under Hun control included the Skirians, the Gepids, the Quadi and the Heruli. The Skirians, at one time a powerful tribe living in southern Russia, were to provide some of the Huns' most valuable auxiliary troops.

The Gepids, like so many of the migratory peoples, came south from Scandinavia. They had a legendary reputation for being lazy. Having had a rendezvous with other Germanic tribes at the mouth of the Vistula, they were reputed to have turned up late through idleness and to have been thereby prevented from taking part in the next migration.[3]

In fact they did reach Dacia in the third century AD. Later they occupied an area in the east of Hungary. Here they encountered the

Huns, with whom they seem to have had a by no means unsatisfactory relationship.

It would be a mistake to suppose that the Huns, as they migrated, all moved in the same direction or that they advanced as a homogeneous whole. There was no unified command before they established their main centres in the Tisza and Danube areas, and some of the Huns followed a very different course from that of the main body.

Among these were the so-called White Huns, who may have acquired the name which posterity still gives them from the writings of the sixth-century Byzantine writer Procopius. 'They are the only ones among the Huns', he stated, 'who have white bodies and countenances which are not ugly.' But he insisted that they were 'of the stock of the Huns in fact as well as in name', adding: 'They do not mingle with any of the Huns known to us, for they occupy a land neither adjoining nor even very near to them.'

This land, which Procopius described as 'goodly', was near the northern frontier of Persia. Once settled there, according to his account, the White Huns ceased to be nomads. He went on: 'They are ruled by one king, and since they possess a lawful constitution, they observe right and justice in their dealings both with one another and with their neighbours, in no degree less than the Romans and the Persians.'

Of the White Huns' social structure Procopius wrote: 'The wealthy citizens are in the habit of attaching to themselves friends to the number of twenty or more, as the case may be, and these become permanently their banquet-companions, and have a share in all their property, enjoying some kind of a common right in this matter.'

There are conflicting accounts of the battles fought between the White Huns and the Persians. The Greek historian Priscus described how a large Hun army, driven by hunger, made a fifteen-day journey and then crossed mountains into Persia. There they devastated much of the land before being met by a superior force and driven back.

Procopius, who, as private secretary to the great commander Belisarius, had first-hand experience of campaigning in Persia, told a different story. According to his account, the Persians attacked the White Huns, who, by pretending to retreat, lured the Persian army into a position from which it could not escape.

The Hun king, whose name Procopius does not give, agreed to spare the Persian army if the Persian king would prostrate himself before him and agree never to attack the Huns again. The Persian king consulted the Magi, who, pointing out that it was the custom of the Persians to prostrate themselves every day before the rising sun, advised him to accept the Huns' terms. This he did, and the Persian army was spared. Not long afterwards, disregarding their oath, the Persians attacked again.

There can be no doubt that people known as Huns caused considerable disruption in the Persian Empire, though their achievements were rather less than were accorded to them by Gibbon when he wrote: 'They advanced, by a secret path, along the shores of the Caspian Sea; traversed the snowy mountains of Armenia; passed the Tigris, the Euphrates and the Halys; recruited their weary cavalry with the generous breed of Cappadocian horses; occupied the hilly country of Cilicia; and disturbed the festal songs and dances of the citizens of Antioch. Egypt trembled at their approach; and the monks and pilgrims of the Holy Land prepared to escape their fury by a speedy embarkation.'

Whether these people should properly be considered Huns is debatable. Procopius's insistence on the striking physical differences between them and other Huns must give rise to doubts. So must some of the social customs which he reported.

On the other hand, recent discoveries of skeletons have shown that only about a quarter of the Huns were of pure Mongolian stock.[4] This very fact makes the use of the term 'Huns' in this connection more plausible. But whatever conclusion may be reached about their racial affinities, it is clear that by their movements the so-called White Huns departed from the main stream of the Hun advance through south-east Europe.

As the main bodies of the Huns continued their advance they encountered after a time a people at a different level of civilization from some of the nomadic tribes with whom they had fought earlier. These were the Ostrogoths, who both practised agriculture to advantage and militarily held sway over a vast area. They had also established an effective monarchy.

The most famous of the Ostrogoth kings, Ermaneric, ruled over territory that extended from the Don to the Dnieper and from the Black

Sea to the Pripet marshes. His repute was such that his name has been preserved for posterity in Germanic legends and chronicles. But not even his forces could effectively resist the Huns.

Realizing that he was facing defeat in battle, Ermaneric decided to take his own life. His successor, Withimir, continued the struggle, but after he was killed in battle effective resistance to the Huns ceased. One more people was added to those who in a variety of ways were obliged to serve the Huns, and through whom the Huns were able to control a massive empire.

By the end of the fourth century the Huns were firmly established along the banks of the Danube which formed the eastern border of the Roman Empire.

CHAPTER 4

THE MAGNET OF EMPIRE

Unlike the earlier Roman Republic the Roman Empire was not an aggressive, expansionist state. Shortly before his death, and after himself completing a series of conquests, the Emperor Augustus advised his step-son and successor, Tiberius, not to extend the frontiers of empire further. With a few exceptions this policy was pursued for some four hundred years.

Britain was effectively conquered in AD 43 and Dacia, a central European territory bounded by the Carpathians and the Danube, by a campaign in 105–6. The Emperor Trajan achieved some spectacular conquests in Asia Minor, but the territorial gains were short-lived. For the rest, Roman military activity was largely confined to the suppression of local rebellion and the protection of frontiers.

Frontier defence was not, for the most part, required because of any threat from other major powers. Indeed, for centuries the only kingdom which the Romans had any need to fear, or to respect militarily, was the Persian Empire of the Sassanids. The day-to-day threat came from peoples who, aware of the peace and relative prosperity which prevailed through much of the Roman Empire, wanted a portion of it for themselves.

The most formidable of these were the Germanic tribes who came from Scandinavia. Among them were the Goths, the Vandals, the Franks and the Burgundians. By the third century AD the Goths had been effectively divided into two separate peoples known as Visigoths and Ostrogoths. The Visigoths occupied territory between the Danube and the Dniester rivers. The Ostrogoths settled east and south of the Dniester.

The Vandals, coming from Jutland, advanced along the Oder and Vistula rivers through territories which today form parts of eastern Germany and Poland. They then turned westward to the Rhine, advanced through Gaul and across the Pyrenees into Spain. Unlike any of the other Germanic peoples, they developed their own navy, which enabled them to dominate much of the littoral of North Africa.

Like 'Hun' the name 'Vandal' and, to a lesser extent, that of 'Goth' have become accepted through Roman usage as terms of abuse. No such opprobrium attaches to the names of the Franks and the Burgundians.

The Franks were also a Germanic tribe. Procopius, the sixth-century Byzantine author of *A History of the Gothic Wars*, wrote of 'the Germans, who are now called Franks.' They were a relatively peaceful people, who had virtually no mounted warriors and occupied territories in what are today Belgium and north-eastern France before advancing further into Gaul.[1] Unlike their more aggressive neighbours they were to establish a dynasty, the Merovingian, which was for long to reign over the territories they occupied at the time of the collapse of the Roman Empire in the west.

The Burgundians, who were mentioned by Pliny the Elder and are believed to have come from the island of Bornholm, settled in the Rhineland. They achieved their greatest fame through a defeat they suffered at the hands of a Hun army in the service of the Romans, a disaster that was to be recorded in the *Nibelungenlied* and other consequent literature.

Rome had created a large free market in which goods circulated easily and in which the roads, the contractors and the soldiery built provided excellent communications. To be a Roman citizen was a valued privilege. When Paul, the Jewish tent-maker from Tarsus, was confronted by a centurion in Jerusalem, who ordered him to be scourged, he said: 'Is it lawful for you to scourge a man that is a Roman and uncondemned?' The centurion was clearly worried and said to his chief captain: 'Take heed what thou doest, for this man is a Roman.' When Paul confirmed that he was indeed a Roman citizen the chief captain said: 'With a great sum obtained I this freedom.' Paul added proudly: 'I was free born.'[2]

That was early in the first century AD. In 212, by the edict of Caracalla, Roman citizenship was accorded to all free inhabitants of the

Empire. The motive of Caracalla, a deplorable character, was no doubt to increase the revenue from the inheritance tax, which only Roman citizens were liable to pay. But the benefits his edict conferred were incalculable. (Caracalla, or Marcus Aurelius Antoninus, as he was more properly named, murdered his brother, ordered a general massacre because he felt he had been treated with disrespect in Alexandria, and suffered from the delusion that he in some way resembled Alexander of Macedon.)

In the Roman Empire a man could be born and live in comfort in Gaul or one of the other provinces, have strong local loyalties, yet proudly proclaim himself a Roman. One such, a single example among countless others, was Decimus Magnus Ausonius, fourth-century poet and man of letters, who was the son of a physician in Bordeaux and who established a school of rhetoric in his home town. Ausonius was chosen to supervise the education of the future Emperor Gratian. Having done so, he returned home to cultivate his vines, translate from the Greek Anthology and write, among other works, a descriptive poem on the beauties of the Moselle river and a series of memorial verses on various Roman emperors.

The Roman Empire's frontiers in Europe were well over two thousand kilometres in length. The legions available to defend it consisted at first of Roman citizens, the auxiliary forces being formed by Roman subjects.

Army life in the outposts of empire was in many ways agreeable. Stone buildings were erected to house the troops, and civilian settlements, including such amenities as bath-houses and amphitheatres, regularly grew up around the camps. One shortcoming – or, to some men perhaps, advantage – of army life was that for a long time marriages contracted by soldiers were not legally valid. But after discharge soldiers could expect adequate arrangements for settling them and their families on the land.[3]

Nevertheless, with growing prosperity, Roman citizens increasingly sought exemption from military duty. Concurrently with this development the requirements of frontier defence became steadily greater. The frontier along the Danube was deemed particularly vulnerable, and a line of forts with look-out posts, stone walls and ditches was gradually built up.

With this and other commitments, the total strength of the Empire's military establishment increased from about 300,000 early in the third century to more than 600,000 some two hundred years later.[4] The increased numbers were achieved largely by allowing some of the barbarians to settle in the Empire in return for undertaking military service as 'federates'.

It was an arrangement which enabled those who would otherwise have been excluded to enjoy the benefits of Roman rule and the Roman economy, while sparing many Roman citizens from what they saw as the tedium and discomfort of military life. As a means of protecting the Empire it might have succeeded much longer than it did but for one factor whose importance could not have been foreseen. This was the arrival of the Huns in the vicinity of the Roman Empire.

The Roman province most immediately threatened by the Huns' advance was known as Pannonia. It included much of what are today eastern Austria and western Hungary as well as parts of Slovenia and Croatia. Its eastern frontier was the Danube. It was designated a Roman province about the beginning of the Christian era. In the reign of the Emperor Trajan it was divided into two parts, Upper and Lower Pannonia.

The capital of Lower Pannonia for a long time was Aquincum, which was near the west bank of the Danube, not far from where Budapest now stands. It was a flourishing city, which by the second century had some sixty thousand inhabitants. In addition to the Roman garrisons and civil administrators and the indigenous population, there were immigrant traders and craftsmen, who had come from various parts of the Empire.

Excavations have shown that the inhabitants of Aquincum enjoyed many of the amenities associated with Roman rule, including public baths, piped water and heating systems. It had a large amphitheatre, and among the discoveries made was a portable organ, which, according to an inscription, had been presented to the guild of firemen.

With all the comforts they enjoyed the inhabitants of Pannonia were made continually conscious that they were living in a frontier town. There were repeated raids in both the third and fourth centuries, when extensive damage was caused. Indeed, in Pannonia as a whole there was a strong tradition of military service. The Danubian armies were by far the largest of any in the Empire, and the region produced numerous generals and aspirants to the imperial throne.

Once it became apparent that a new threat to parts of Pannonia had come with the arrival of the Huns, elaborate efforts were made to strengthen the frontier defences. Citizens were conscripted to build walls and take food to people in areas afflicted by raids. A survey of all points where the frontier might be crossed was instituted, and a major boat-building programme was undertaken in order to strengthen the Danube fleet. The aim was to have two hundred vessels in service at the end of seven years. Local officials were to be fined if they failed to fulfil the tasks allotted to them.[5]

The first of the Hun military leaders known to have posed any threat to the Empire was called Balamber, but he remains a rather shadowy figure. Of Uldin, who effected crossings of the Danube with success in the first years of the fifth century, rather more is known. Zosimus described him as 'the Prince of the Huns', and he is known to have commanded a considerable force, which included not only Huns but a large body of Skirians.[6]

He was evidently ambitious. A contemporary historian, the fifth-century Constantinople lawyer Hermias Salamenes Sozomenus, generally known as Sozomen, described what happened when Uldin was approached by some imperial emissaries. In rejecting the terms they offered he pointed to the rising sun and said that the conquest of the Huns would extend as far as the sun's course.

Uldin also had a taste for the macabre. This was shown when the ambitious and controversial soldier-politician Gainas fell into his hands. During the reign of the youthful Emperor Arcadius, of whom it was said that he always looked as if he was about to fall asleep, his chief minister Rufinus was killed by Gainas during a review of troops in the Emperor's presence.

Arcadius reacted to this coup by appointing a eunuch named Eutropius in Rufinus's place and by making Gainas, who was a soldier and a Goth, the commander of the armies of the Empire in the east. Gainas became increasingly unpopular. Riots broke out in Constantinople, which may have been directed against Goths generally as much as against Gainas personally. Some seven thousand people were reported to have been killed, and Gainas, who was still outside the city, was prevented from entering.

He then led a somewhat peripatetic existence at the head of a mercenary force. In time he reached the Danube, where he was captured by the Huns. Uldin had him beheaded and sent his head to Arcadius in Constantinople.

What followed in the half-century after Uldin's crossing of the Danube is the story of how a people who were gifted yet ignorant, predatory yet in many ways tolerant, and who acquired an inspired leader, responded when confronted by the power of the greatest empire on earth. It is also the story of how that empire responded to the importunities of the Huns.

CHAPTER 5

ATTILA BECOMES KING OF THE HUNS

The first of the Hun rulers of whom we have any detailed knowledge was named Ruga. He was a powerful king, but how absolute his dominion over the Huns was is questionable. The consolidation of the various tribes into a single kingdom was a gradual process, which had probably not been completed in Ruga's time. Ruga had a brother named Mundzuk, who had two sons, Bleda and Attila.[1]

A Constantinople author named Olympiodorus, whose twelve-volume history has unfortunately been lost, described, for example, a mission in which he himself took part in 412 to a Hun king who was given the Roman name of Donatus. The outcome of the mission was that the emissaries, after exchanging oaths of friendship with Donatus, had him murdered. As the mission to Donatus sailed northward across the Black Sea it is evident that his realm lay well to the east of that of Ruga.[2]

In 422 Ruga, taking advantage of the withdrawal of imperial forces to combat a threat from Persia, decided to launch an attack along the lower Danube. From there his forces advanced into Thrace. A settlement was reached with the government of Theodosius II, in which it was agreed that the Huns would receive an annual tribute of 350 pounds of gold, or 25,200 solidi, in return for keeping the peace.

Latter-day historians have condemned Theodosius and his advisers for poltroonery in adopting a policy of trying to buy peace from Hun invaders, but they had to consider the relative merits of losing gold or losing manpower. They knew that plunder was necessary to the Hun economy and that much of the gold would be spent in acquiring goods from the more prosperous parts of the Empire. In some respects the policy did not greatly differ from that known today as overseas aid.

Ruga also showed exceptional skill in his dealings with the Empire in the west. Already in Uldin's time the Huns had adopted the practice of holding the young sons of prominent Romans hostage as a means of applying pressure. One of these hostages was named Aetius, who was to become a military commander of outstanding distinction and whose path in life was repeatedly to cross that of Attila.

Aetius acquired a good understanding of Hun society and is believed to have spoken the Hun language. He became friendly with Ruga, and they both exploited their association to advantage.

Their collaboration began when Aetius asked for Hun troops to help him in an internal conflict in Italy. The troops were provided, and from then on Aetius, who was to become the most powerful man in the west other than the Emperor, was increasingly dependent on Hun soldiery.

In return for these services Aetius negotiated a treaty in 433, whereby a part of Pannonia, known as Pannonia Secunda, was ceded to the Huns. For Ruga this was a considerable diplomatic triumph. The Huns, for so long a nomadic people, now had a permanent home, a change which clearly affected their lifestyle and culture.

Ruga died in 434 and was succeeded by Bleda, Attila's elder brother. Some confusion has been caused by a traditional belief, fostered perhaps by those who wanted to magnify Attila, that Bleda and Attila were joint rulers from the time of Ruga's death.

This is almost certainly incorrect. Bleda established his headquarters in the lower Tisza area. Attila's was further down the Danube in the Bucharest-Ploesti region. Attila was a powerful prince, enjoying considerable independence, but his status was that of second-in-command to Bleda.[3]

The death of Ruga seems to have been regarded in Constantinople as an excuse for suspending the agreement he had reached with the Huns. Bleda thought otherwise and demanded a meeting with plenipotentiary ambassadors.

The meeting took place near Margus (today Orasje near Dubrovica) on the Morava river, which flows south through Serbia. Bleda and Attila pitched their richly decorated tents opposite the Roman fortress and insisted on negotiating on horseback.

To this condition the emissaries from Constantinople, whose names were Plinthas and Epigenes, were obliged to agree. They also accepted all the Huns' terms, the Empire undertaking to double the annual tribute from 350 pounds of gold to 700 and agreeing not to enter into any alliances with enemies of the Huns and to repudiate such alliances as already existed.

Other conditions agreed were the establishment of a free market on the banks of the Danube, which was guaranteed by both sides, and the handing over by the Emperor's government of all Huns whom it held. Some were prisoners of war, others were fugitives. Huns of both categories readily served in the imperial forces.

The treaty of Margus of 435 was for the Huns an unqualified triumph. The insistence on negotiating on horseback was a form of panache, for Attila was later to show himself quite capable of conducting similar negotiations while seated in a palace, but it made a lasting impression.

The gains were substantial, for the Huns were not, as in the past, making demands simply as a result of successful raids, but were imposing conditions for the security of their kingdom and the benefit of their economy.

As a consequence of the treaty Bleda and Attila were able to direct their attention away from the Balkans and to consolidate their empire in the direction of the Alps and the Rhine. This they did with outstanding success, in particular through campaigns against Germanic peoples.[4]

In 439 and 440 wars affecting the Empire broke out on a number of fronts. In October 439 the Vandals occupied Carthage, which, having arisen from the total destruction inflicted by Roman Republican forces, had again become a city of major importance. The next year substantial forces were sent from both the Eastern and Western Empires for the defence of Sicily against the Vandals. The Persians then attacked Armenia.

Enough intelligence of what was happening reached Bleda to convince him that he again had an opportunity of plundering the Balkans.

The first news the Imperial Government had that the Huns were once more in action was a report of a successful attack on the Roman fortress known as Castra Constantia on the Danube. This was coupled with an assault on the nearby market-place, where all the traders were seized.

The Huns' action was a clear breach of the treaty of Margus, which had provided for the operation of a free market in this neighbourhood. The justification that the Huns offered was the claim that the Bishop of Margus had surreptitiously entered their territory and robbed the graves of Hun kings of treasures that had been buried with them.

Surprisingly, perhaps, the Roman emissaries with whom the Huns treated do not seem to have denied this charge. Nor had they any answer to the much more plausible claim that a large number of fugitives from the Hun empire were still being retained in spite of the provisions of the treaty of Margus.

The immediate Hun demands were the surrender of the Bishop of Margus and of the fugitive Huns, and when neither was met, military action followed.

Bleda's campaign, in which Attila played at most a minor part, was conducted in two stages. In 440 a limited operation led to the capture of Viminiacum, now the Serbian town of Kostolac, after which there was a brief truce. Hostilities were resumed the next year.[5]

The first objective in the 441 campaign was Margus. Here the Bishop, who, in Gibbon's words, 'did not possess the spirit of a martyr', played a significant role. Realizing that the Huns were not going to be deflected, he entered into negotiations with them, received assurances of his free-dom – assurances that were duly kept – and was reported to have opened the gates of the city with his own hands.[6]

The Huns were then able to advance southward with, it seems, little opposition and captured Constantine's birthplace, Nish or Naissus. Sofia (Serdica) and Plovdiv (Philoppolis) also fell. Certain fortresses held out, such as Edirne (Hadrianople) and Iregli (Heracleia), but Hun forces reached the sea at three points. They presented no serious threat to Constantinople itself, but they had achieved enough to insist on a new treaty.

The negotiations were carried out this time by the Supreme Com-mander of the Eastern Army and Consul-Senator Anatolius. The annual tribute in gold was again increased, and back-payment for two years at the higher level was also made. New assurances were given on the handing over of Hun prisoners, deserters or refugees.

That the triumph was primarily Bleda's, not Attila's, has been deduced – probably rightly – from evidence that in 441 Attila was still considering whether he ought to be involved in the fighting, and that after it had been going on for some time he was in correspondence with the government in Constantinople.

In this he made the familiar demands for the payment of tribute and the return of some Hun nobles, and negotiations were conducted at his headquarters. When his demands were not met, he too attacked some imperial fortresses with success. But this seems to have been an independent action, and only after it are Attila's forces thought to have joined in the main war conducted under Bleda's command.

In 443 Bleda died. The cause of his death is a mystery that never has been, and never can be, solved. Different theories became established in legend.

One, which is not very convincing, was that Bleda, not being interested in affairs of state and leaving Attila to deal with them, occupied himself mainly with hunting, and that it was in a hunting accident that he was killed. Another belief, which took stronger root, was that Attila had Bleda murdered.

Either version may be true. Accidental deaths and deaths from natural causes of prominent people have been disbelieved, though true, in all ages. It is also possible, indeed likely, that there was a power struggle between Bleda and Attila.

A man of Attila's commanding personality would not have relished remaining a second-in-command indefinitely. It is possible that Bleda, realizing this, thought it would be prudent to remove him and Attila acted in self-defence. It is equally possible that Attila organized a coup d'état and deliberately had Bleda killed.

Documentary information about Bleda is slight, though he and Attila were known to have had disagreements. One of these involved a dwarf named Zerko, who had belonged to the imperial general Aspar. Zerko became a captive of the Huns, and Bleda found him a continual source of amusement. He even provided him with a Hun wife.

Attila actively disliked Zerko and after Bleda's death presented him to Aetius, who in turn gave him back to Aspar. When Zerko wanted to have his Hun wife sent to him Attila refused.

The importance attached to this apparently minor difference between the two brothers by those who related the story to a contemporary chronicler suggests that it may have been one of many.[7] But of the true relationship between the brothers too little is known for any pronouncement on the cause of Bleda's death to be other than speculative.

What is certain is that after Bleda's death there were no further suggestions of dual or divided control. Attila was acknowledged without question as the sole King of the Huns. He was the first man who could make that claim with absolute assurance. He was also to be the last.

CHAPTER 6

ATTILA'S KINGDOM

As a ruler Attila was an originator, in some respects a revolutionary. He clearly perceived that if the Huns were to become a great power, as he intended them to be, they must learn from other more advanced peoples. His own intimate circle of advisers, in consequence, consisted largely of foreigners.

One of these, Orestes, was married to the daughter of the military commander of the Roman province of Noricum. Bringing his wife with him, he came to Attila's court to offer his services. He occupied a prominent position from then on. His son Romulus became the last of the Roman Emperors in the West.

Attila's principal secretary, Constantius, came from Italy. Another man of consequence to make his way to Attila's court and, once there, to exercise influence, was a former doctor named Eudoxius. Earlier in his life he had led a peasant rising in the Loire region.

Two other prominent figures in Attila's entourage were brothers. Their racial origins are uncertain, but they were Hellenized in their culture. One of them, Onegesius, became a kind of court chamberlain or vizier. The other, Scotta, had been instructed by Attila to collect the gold and the Hun fugitives stipulated in the terms of the treaty agreed by Anatolius. He was able to bring back the gold, but the Huns, he discovered, had nearly all been massacred.

Such men knew the outside world and spoke as their mother tongue one of the two principal languages of the Empire, Latin, which prevailed in the West, or Greek, which was the common language of the East.

Hun society was polygamous, the rulers having a number of wives. The first wife was accorded clear precedence over the others, her offspring normally enjoying a similar distinction. There was an aristocracy of birth, privileges passing from father to son. Court etiquette in the time of Attila was elaborate, and there is strong evidence that the rules of this were formulated over a long period. Archaeological finds have suggested the prevalence of what has been described as 'a powerful Central-Asian-cum-Persian culture, in which decoration and etiquette played a powerful part.'[1]

Contemporary accounts show that the luxuries enjoyed by the Hun ruling class included gold and silver ornaments, Indian pearls, silks, dates from Phoenicia and Indian pepper. Some of these were no doubt acquired as plunder, but others must have come by way of trade. So far as is known, the principal export which the Huns had to offer was horses.

Hun graves in different areas reveal fine craftsmanship in the making of bridles and saddles as well as bows and arrows. Some of the swords are as long as 120 centimetres, and some have elaborately carved gold handles.[2] Warriors of exceptional distinction were sometimes buried with golden bows.

There are copper and bronze vessels of Hun origin, and some of the ceramic work shows evidence of Chinese influence.

By the middle of the fifth century Huns of the upper classes had their own wooden houses in the villages. If one is to judge by a written description of Attila's palace, it may be assumed that the rooms were screened off from one another by tapestries.[3]

Many of the conquered peoples became slaves of the Huns. When Hun nobles went to war their retinues might consist equally of slaves and free men. As in the Roman Empire there were opportunities for slaves to obtain their freedom, and there is at least one recorded instance of a foreign slave of the Huns becoming a rich man after obtaining his freedom under the rule of Attila.[4]

When the Huns occupied a new territory large numbers of people fled before them, but the numbers of those who remained were larger still. Many of those who stayed were agriculturists, and the Huns not only allowed them to continue to till the land, but encouraged them to do so. The economy of the territory depended largely on the work of these people.

For example, agricultural produce of the Gepids under Hun dominion included wheat, barley, rye, peas and various forms of fruit. The contemporary account we have of a visit to Attila's capital indicates that wine was freely offered to guests. The lower orders drank mead, beer and cherry juice, but there is evidence to suggest that wine was not the exclusive privilege of the ruling class. Nor indeed was the eating of meat, particularly mutton.

The Huns became a kind of military ruling class or aristocracy in the territories that they successfully invaded. To what extent their rule was a benign one is open to question, but there is no evidence to suggest that it was in any way more cruel than that of other contemporary conquerors.

Of the Hun language virtually nothing is known. In the middle of the sixth century Procopius described the Huns as 'absolutely unacquainted with writing and unskilled in it to the present day.' Scholars have attempted to deduce the provenance of Hun proper names, but there is no clear agreement even on the group of languages to which Hunnic should be assigned.[5]

More has been written on the religion of the Huns, an informative source being the Armenian chronicler Moses Daskhuranci. He was no admirer of the Huns and was dismissive of what he called their 'satanically deluded tree-worshipping errors.' But he described in some detail how the Huns offered horses as burnt offerings to a deity, whom one modern authority has identified with a god known to have been worshipped by the Hsiung-Nu in Mongolia.[6] Daskhuranci also wrote of the Hun practice of lacerating their faces as a sign of mourning. First-hand descriptions of the appearance of some Huns give support to this assertion.

Animals certainly played an important part in the Hun religion, just as they did in their daily lives. Horses' skulls were commonly placed on poles in front of dwelling places to ward off evil. The wolverene, an exceptionally pugnacious animal, served as a war totem and the bear as a peace totem. The choice of the bear has been explained on the ground that, whereas she-bears can be frightening, the males of the species always appear amiable.[7]

The Huns did not practise cremation, but buried their dead – at least their noble dead – with objects believed to be of value to them in the after-life. Among such objects were swords, which even in a warrior's lifetime might acquire a mystic quality.

That the outstanding figures among the Huns believed fervently in their religion seems more than probable. Attila certainly paid close attention to the pronouncements of his priests or soothsayers and allowed them to influence his military decisions. In this he did not differ from Greeks or Romans who had preceded him or Christians or Muslims who would follow.

For more than a century after the establishment of Christianity as the official faith of the Roman Empire, there were no organized efforts to spread the gospel outside the Empire's frontiers. Conversions did take place among those who dwelt outside, but these were a consequence of persuasion – and example – by Christians who had been captured in war and enslaved.

Within the Empire, Christianity spread rapidly among the Gothic peoples with whom the Huns were periodically in contact. Missionary work was particularly successful among the Visigoths, not least through the efforts of the son – or possibly grandson – of a Roman who had been made prisoner. The name by which he is now known, Ulfila, was probably a contraction of a Gothic word meaning 'little wolf'.

In 332, when he was still in his early twenties, Ulfila was sent, possibly as a hostage, to Constantinople. There he came into contact with a number of religious leaders and accepted a doctrine later to be condemned as heresy. In 341, by now a bishop, he returned to serve as a missionary among the Visigoths for some forty years.

In the course of his duties he translated the Bible into Gothic. Unfortunately only a fragment of it remains, the manuscript being housed today in the University of Uppsala. Its arrival there was a consequence of the last of the raids by Scandinavians into Central Europe. In 1648 it was removed by Swedish soldiers from Prague. It was later presented to Queen Christina.

The doctrine that Ulfila preached among the Visigoths was Arianism. Its name was derived from the teachings of Arius, a deacon in Alexandria, who received his theological education in Antioch. A man of impressive appearance, he was an inspired propagandist, even expressing his opinions in what became the popular songs of the day. But authority was against him, and in his last years in Constantinople he was seen as an old, sick and manifestly harmless figure, pleading to be allowed the benefit of the sacraments.[8]

Arius seems to have been concerned with logic rather than revelation. When considering the relationships between God the Father and God the Son, he argued that the Son, being created later than the Father, must therefore be inferior. His aim, he declared, was to establish the unity and simplicity of the eternal God.

At the Council of Nicaea held in 325 under the direction of the Emperor Constantine it was decided that the Son was of the same substance as the Father and it was a logical step from this to condemn Arianism as heresy.

It has been argued plausibly that the appeal of Arianism to the Germanic tribes within the Empire was enhanced because they could relate the concept of a Son, who was not quite equal to the supreme God, to their own traditions of demi-gods.[9] It is likely too that if the Huns had become baptized in large numbers in the fourth or fifth centuries it would have been in the Arian form of the faith.

In fact Christian missionaries made little headway among the Huns. A bishop named Theotimus was reported to have been held in high esteem by Huns living near the Danube, who even referred to him as 'the god of the Romans'.[10] There were Hun prisoners who were converted to Christianity, and no doubt the religion spread here and there among the Huns in other ways.

There is no evidence of persecution of Christians as such by Attila or his predecessors. Indeed, it is clear from contemporary documentation that Christians in the Hun empire were free to practise their faith. But there was no mass conversion of Huns before the seventh century.

This was certainly one of the reasons why contemporary and near-contemporary chroniclers in general wrote so disparagingly about the Huns.

In both the Hun economy and Hun decorative arts gold played an important part. During the fifth century, which some archaeologists have even described as 'the golden age', it came into the possession of the Huns in the form of tribute in large quantities. But the amount of Hun gold to be seen in Hungary today is surprisingly small. One reason for this is the curious manner in which much of it came to light.

In 1926 a peasant woman brought a piece of gold to a jeweller in Szeged. She explained that it had been found in a vineyard in the vicinity of Nagyszeksos. The jeweller thought it interesting and took it to the director of the Szeged Museum.

The director at that time was Ferenc Mora, one of Hungary's leading men of letters, a prolific writer, novelist, polemicist and poet. One of his best known works, *The Golden Coffin*, was set in the time of the Roman Emperor Diocletian.

Mora quickly identified the object as a Hun artefact and tried to persuade the jeweller, the peasant woman and anyone else who was aware of the discovery to keep it secret. In this he had limited success, but he immediately initiated a scientific exploration of the vineyard and adjoining territory.

In the late 1920s and early 1930s some hundreds of gold objects were discovered in the area. They included drinking vessels, torques, daggers, knives and horses' harnesses.[11] Many of them were found near the surface, and in the course of the explorations it was learnt that for a long time, perhaps for generations, the local peasantry had been helping themselves to Hun gold whenever they were in need of money. As had happened on the same territory fifteen hundred and more years earlier, gold was being used as a convenient means of barter.

Some of these Hun treasures are said to have emerged in museums in western Europe, where their provenance has not always been recognized. Those which, through Ferenc Mora's efforts, were housed in the Szeged Museum have been afforded an unusual degree of protection.

Towards the end of World War II, when the Soviet armies entered Hungary, the new director of the Szeged Museum decided that his first duty was to protect the Hun gold from possible new predators. He therefore set out on foot northwards with a wheelbarrow, in which he had placed the gold, the museum typewriter and a few personal possessions. In the course of his journey he was relieved by the Soviet soldiery of the typewriter and his personal possessions, including his overcoat. But the Hun gold was concealed under some sandwiches, which had become so mouldy that they excited no interest.

The director succeeded in reaching the Austrian frontier and later, when military movements had become less fluid, he was able to return with the gold to Szeged. There he was charged by the Soviet-controlled government with removing national treasures to a foreign country, and was replaced by an official deemed more politically correct.

Today the golden objects of the Huns are kept in a vault in the Szeged Museum. There they can be seen by the privileged as abiding relics of an economy in which plunder and tribute played leading parts.[12]

CHAPTER 7

THE THREAT TO CONSTANTINOPLE

It has been suggested that one reason why Attila surrounded himself with foreigners was that after Bleda's death he no longer trusted prominent Huns and they no longer trusted him.[1] There may be some truth in this, but his principal motive was, almost certainly, his determination to raise standards in his kingdom to the level of those prevailing elsewhere, so that he could treat with the mightiest rulers as equals. In this respect a comparison with Peter the Great of Russia is not altogether inapt.

The great German nineteenth-century historian Theodor Mommsen was of the opinion that Attila's greatest achievement was his strengthening of central authority over the Huns. Attila's kingdom was not, as the Hun empire had earlier been, an association of tribes under one main ruler. It was governed from a central court, as was the Roman Empire. Attila himself could go campaigning in a variety of countries, as Roman Emperors repeatedly did, but authority rested with him wherever he was. By his employment of competent foreigners he laid the foundations of what might have developed into an efficient civil service.

Attila also understood that for military successes of the kind he envisaged he would need the consistent support of peoples other than the Huns. In particular he looked for help to the Skirians and the Gepids, with whose kings he had established a close relationship. The King of the Gepids, Ardaric, was to prove his most reliable ally. His trust in the Skirian King, Edika, seemed at one stage to have been not so well placed. It is possible that the alliance of the three men had been decisive in ensuring that at the time of Bleda's death Attila came to power successfully.

Attila's first major military campaign was, like those of Ruga and Bleda, in the Balkans, but in both concept and execution it differed appreciably from traditional Hun methods of waging war. No longer was strategy based, almost entirely, on lightning strikes by horsemen appearing as if from nowhere, advancing, feigning retreat, recovering, and all the time darkening the sky with arrows.

Such methods had been extraordinarily effective in campaigns through sparsely inhabited countryside or even in the capture of lightly fortified towns with, perhaps, only one defensive tower. Attila was more ambitious. His objective was Constantinople itself, and his method was to advance with a large expeditionary force, of which Germanic and Iranian peoples formed a considerable part.

The new invasion took place in 447, the army's route being rather further to the east than in the preceding campaign. In this way a number of new fortifications were by-passed. Progress was slower than before and destruction considerably greater. An ecclesiastical chronicler, Callinicus, author of a biography of St Hypatius, wrote of the new campaign: 'The barbarian nation of the Huns, which was in Thrace, became so great that more than a hundred cities were captured. There were so many murders and blood-lettings that the dead could not be numbered. Ay, for they took captive the churches and monasteries and slew the monks and maidens in great quantities.' Callinicus was no doubt a prejudiced commentator, but it may be significant that an earlier chronicler had stated that until then the Huns had not destroyed monasteries, killed monks and nuns, or desecrated the graves of saints.[2]

Against Callinicus's figure of a hundred, others have estimated the number of cities captured by Attila's army to have been about seventy. Whatever the truth may have been, the campaign was evidently conducted with a thoroughness not shown by Hun armies before, and from time to time detours were made so that additional cities could be captured and destroyed. One such was Sofia, or Serdica, on whose ruins a Slav people would later build a new city.

In Constantinople news of the army's advance caused growing concern. This turned to consternation when, on the morning of 26 January 447, the worst earthquake of which there was, until then, any record in the Bosphorus region occurred. It was followed by some four days and nights of continuous rain. Countless buildings were destroyed, hillocks were levelled, rivers of water poured through the city, and there was an epidemic of plague.

Most serious of all, so far as the defence of the city was affected, was the damage done to the walls. No fewer than fifty-seven of the towers were destroyed, and gaping holes were left, through which an enemy could easily advance.

Panic was widespread for a time, but the Praetorian Prefect, Flavius Constantinus, decided that the most pressing task, even where there was so much loss of life and damage to property, was the rebuilding of the walls.

As in Rome, chariot-racing was watched by the people of Constantinople with passionate interest, and the supporters of different factions were divided into four bodies known as Blues, Whites, Greens and Reds. Constantinus wisely decided to mobilize these bodies and put them to the task of restoring the walls, no doubt on a competitive basis. The work was completed in the astonishingly short time of two months, and the defences were made even stronger than they had been before.

At almost any time during those two months Attila's army, had it been near enough, might well have captured the city. Had he adopted the traditional Hun tactics of the blitzkrieg, the opportunity might have presented itself. But he did not. The army advanced slowly, pillaging and destroying. Nevertheless, to the people of Constantinople, even after their walls had been repaired, the danger was still evident.

As the invading army approached, many people fled from the city. There were rumours that Theodosius himself was about to follow their example. In fact he stayed, but there was little popular confidence in Flavius Zeno, the man entrusted with the immediate defence of the capital.[3]

There was, however, another commander appointed by Theodosius. He was a German named Arnegliscus, who decided that, rather than wait for Attila's army to make a frontal assault on the city, he would join battle at some distance outside.

A major engagement took place in Thrace. Arnegliscus fought with a courage that impressed those who witnessed it, but he was killed in action. Attila's army suffered heavy losses, but could reasonably claim a victory. Marcianople, then the largest city in Thrace and the base from which Arnegliscus had operated, was captured and destroyed, and Attila's army was freed to devastate much of Greece. It even advanced as far as Thermopylae, where a Persian army had long before been resisted.

Attila did not make a serious assault on Constantinople. No doubt he appreciated that he did not have the armoury to break down the newly repaired walls. He was also confronted with a problem which he would later have to face in an even more acute form. This was disease among his troops.

Malaria, which had such devastating consequences in the later centuries of the Roman Empire, was probably one of the afflictions. Contemporary evidence suggests that dysentery was another. This evidence is to be found in the work of Isaac of Antioch, who wrote a 'Homily on the Royal City', in which he addressed the Emperor in the second person.

God, he declared, 'conquered the tyrant who was threatening to come and take thee away captive. Against the stone of sickness they stumbled and the steeds fell and their riders, and the camp which was prepared for thy destruction was silenced. Through sickness he laid low the Huns who threatened thee. The sinners drew the bow and put their arrows on the string – and preparation had perfected itself and the host was on the point of coming quickly – then sickness blew through it and hurled the host into wilderness. He whose heart was strong for battle waxed feeble through sickness. He who was skilled in shooting with the bow, sickness of the bowels overthrew him – the riders of the steed slumbered and slept and the cruel army was silenced.'[4]

The army was only halted by sickness. It was not destroyed, and Attila remained a perpetual menace to the well-being and security of Constantinople itself and, indeed, of the whole of the Eastern Empire. Knowing this, he continually increased his demands.

The annual tribute had already been raised to six thousand pounds of gold by the treaty agreed with Anatolius, and as Attila sent one emissary after another calling for new exactions, the threat to Theodosius's economy became serious. He was no longer confronted simply with the problem of how best to cope with the periodic importunities of plundering barbarians. The cost of a major war had substantially diminished the treasury, and new money had to be raised.

A tax was even imposed on senators, and to meet it some of them had to sell their wives' jewellery and family heirlooms. St John Chrysostom, in one of his verbal onslaughts on the luxury prevailing in Constantinople, stated that every rich household had a large semi-circular table of silver so heavy that two men could barely lift it and a huge, solid gold vase in addition to gold cups and dishes. Much of this now went into the melting-pot.

Attila repeated, more implacably than ever, his demands for the release of all Hun prisoners. He also insisted on the handing over of men of any race who had transferred their loyalty from the Huns to the Empire. A number of such men chose death at the hands of imperial officers rather than return to the Huns, and the prestige of an imperial army which was unable to protect its own recruits plummeted disastrously.[5]

Other demands were territorial. Attila now called for the release from imperial rule of a stretch of territory some five hundred kilometres wide around the lower Danube. One effect of this would have been to place the border town with the free market, which the Huns required, as far south as Nish.

This last demand was considered excessive, and it became clear to those in power in Constantinople that there could be no lasting peace as long as Attila was still alive.

CHAPTER 8

THE CITY CONSTANTINE BUILT

To understand the magnitude of the task that Attila set himself in attacking the Roman Empire it is necessary to consider how that empire had developed in the late fourth and early fifth centuries. In particular we have to take into account how it came to be divided into two parts and how and why the city of Constantinople was built.

The division of the Roman Empire into east and west was a gradual process, its official recognition following long after it had become a demonstrable fact. A powerful impetus to the division was given by the Emperor Diocletian, an innovator, the magnitude of whose reforms of empire was matched, or exceeded, only by those of Augustus and Constantine the Great.

Diocletian, who was proclaimed Emperor in AD 284, was a soldier of peasant origin from a part of Dalmatia in the Roman province of Illyria. The majority of Roman Emperors were primarily military men, a fact which posterity has tended to overlook, possibly because of the peculiar eccentricities of a small number of exceptional Emperors such as Nero, Caracalla and Heliogabalus.

As a soldier, Diocletian reached the conclusion that the Empire, as it was constituted when he assumed power, was almost ungovernable. All the important threats came from the east. The country that the Romans had once known as Parthia, and from which they long had little to fear, had fallen under the control of the warlike dynasty of the Sassanids, the creators of a new Persian Empire, who claimed the title of 'King of the Kings of the Iranians and non-Iranians'.

The Persian army had a much better understanding of the use of cavalry than was normally attained by the Romans, with their tradition of advances by infantry under the tortoise-like cover provided by shields. Over the years Valerian, Julian and Jovian were to be among the emperors who suffered capture, death or surrender when confronted by Persian armies. Valerian, during a long period of captivity, was even subjected to continuous physical humiliations.

Cross-border raids by nomadic or other tribes offered, before the fifth century, a much less serious military threat than did the Persians, but the Danube was a long frontier to man and patrol effectively. On military grounds, therefore, Diocletian was fully justified in establishing the effective capital of the Roman Empire where the Turkish town of Izmit, on the Sea of Marmora, now stands. It was then known as Nicomedia.

To assist him in governing his huge empire Diocletian appointed another soldier, Maximian, as co-emperor, or second Augustus, thus establishing the system of dual control. He then went further and appointed two deputies, known as Caesars, and divided the Empire into four prefectures. The choice of their capitals was significant. In addition to Izmit (or Nicomedia) they were Milan, Trier and Mitrovica, which was then known as Sirmium and is near the present border between Serbia and Croatia. Only one of these cities, Milan, was in Italy, and that was in the north. Rome was not included.

Among Diocletian's other major reforms were an overhaul of the system of taxation, improvements in the mobility of the army, and the establishment of a new kind of centralized civil service. Having completed his work, he chose to abdicate and live in his splendid palace at Split on the Dalmatian coast. He had by then reached the conclusion that he would derive more pleasure from growing cabbages than from ruling an empire.

Diocletian's system of dual control survived, with one emperor established in the east and one in the west. The experiment of having four rulers was short-lived. Its effect was to create an excessive number of claimants to the imperial throne and to give rise to clashes between what amounted to their private armies. The Emperor Constantine, who attained supreme power in 306, could do so only after defeating one rival after another.

Constantine's early military career might have suggested that, if he were to become Emperor at all, it would be in the west. He was first proclaimed Emperor by the army in Britain after his father had died in York. On attaining undisputed control he did in fact visit Rome, but he soon made it clear that he had no intention of living there.

Constantine had been converted to the Christian faith while campaigning. Rome was not only the home of the Senate but also the site of ancient pagan cults. Neither of these appealed to Constantine. The Senate, although its powers had been steadily eroded, embodied traditions of government firmly opposed to the absolutism towards which Diocletian's reforms of the administration had pointed, and which Constantine himself favoured. The pagan cults offended his new-found faith.

Constantine considered the possibility of creating a new capital in Nish in Serbia, then known as Naissus, which was his birthplace. This was, and has long been, an important centre of communications, commanding, as it does, two valleys that lead from Central Europe towards the Aegean. But it was not easily defensible, as Attila was to show. Nicomedia was another possibility, for Constantine had lived there in his youth, when he had been held as a hostage at the court of Diocletian to ensure that his father remained loyal to the Emperor.

In the end Constantine's choice was Byzantium, whose strategic advantages were readily apparent to him. Situated on a hilly promontory, with the Sea of Marmora to the south, and the bay of the Bosphorus, including the wonderful natural harbour known as the Golden Horn, to the north, it was almost impregnable to attack from the sea. Hills and the narrowness of the promontory made it easily defensible against land forces.

Byzantium was already an important trading centre, where Greek colonists had long prospered and levies had been imposed on ships passing to and from the Black Sea. For a variety of compelling reasons it seemed to Constantine the right choice for a city which he designated New Rome.

From the outset Constantine made it clear that he intended to build a city that would not only be a rival to Rome, the most populous and splendid city that man had yet created, but which, wherever possible, would surpass it. To achieve his ends he brought treasures from cities in different parts of the Empire. 'Constantinople dedicated: almost every other city stripped naked,' St Jerome commented laconically.

The south-eastern part of the town of Byzantium was chosen as the site of Constantine's palace, all existing houses covering a large area being first demolished. To the north-west of the palace a forum between three and four hundred metres in length was built. It was paved with marble and surrounded by impressive buildings. The principal market-place was situated just outside the old walls. Here a golden milestone was erected, from which distances to outlying places would thenceforward be measured.[1]

In the sixteenth century a remarkable document reached western Europe for the first time. It contained 'a detailed description of the city of Constantinople as it stood in the reigns of Arcadius and Honorius' – that is to say in the first decades of the fifth century AD.

It had been translated by a native of Albi, who called himself Petrus Gyllius, and who had been sent by King Francis I of France to Italy and Greece to collect ancient manuscripts. It was later translated into English and published in London in 1729. Since then it has been surprisingly neglected.[2]

Constantinople, as the author of this document explained, was divided into fourteen regions or wards. He went on to describe them in detail. The first ward contained 'the house of Placidia Augusta; the house of the most illustrious Marina; the bagnios of Arcadius; 29 streets; 118 large houses; two porticoes of a great length; fifteen private bagnios; four public and fifteen private mills; and four gradus.'

The word 'gradus', it was explained, 'signifies a tribunal, which was ascended by marble steps to receive the bread which was distributed among the common people and which was therefore called panis gradilis.' Another of the author's comments was: 'I take the word houses in this place to signify the dwelling houses of some of the principal men of the city distinguished by standing by themselves and having no other houses adjoining to them.'

This first ward was far from being the most splendid. 'The second ward,' the author wrote, 'after an easy and almost imperceptible ascent above its level from the lesser theatre, falls with a deep precipice down to the sea. This ward contains in it the great church of St Sophia; the old church; the senate house; a tribunal with porphyry steps; the bagnios of Zeuxippus; a theatre; an amphitheatre; 34 streets; 98 large houses; four great porticoes; thirteen private baths; four private mills and four gradus.'

A feature of this ward which particularly attracted the author's attention was not St Sophia, nor the senate house, nor the amphitheatre, but the baths of Zeuxippus. 'In this bagnio', he wrote, 'there was a pleasant variety of prospects of surprising art, both in marble and in stonework, in statues of brass, and figures of persons of antiquity, who seemed to want nothing but a soul to animate and enliven them.

'Among these celebrated pieces of the most excellent workmanship was the statue of old Homer in a thoughtful posture, just as he was, his hands folded in his breast, his beard carefully hanging down, his hair very thin before, his face wrinkled with age and the cares of the world; his nose well proportioned; his eyes fixed in their sockets, as is usual with blind persons, which he was generally looked upon to be.'

Ward after ward was described in similar detail, and the author also explained how the safety and well-being of their inhabitants was assured. Each ward, he wrote, 'was governed by one curator, who had under his charge the whole ward. There was also the Vernaculus, who was messenger of the ward, was also assistant to him, and entirely at his command. It had also twenty-five Collegiati, chosen out of the several bodies of tradesmen, whose office it was to direct and assist in cases of fire. There were also five Vico-Magistri, whose business it was to watch the city by night.'

Of Constantine the Great the author wrote that he 'built several forums, some as an ornament, some for the service of the city. The hippodrome he beautified with temples, fountains, porticoes and a senate house and allowed its members equal honours and privileges with those of Rome.

'He also built himself a palace, little inferior to the royal one at Rome. In short he was so ambitious to make it rival Rome itself in all its grandeur and magnificence that at length, as Sozomen assures us, it far surpassed it, both in the number of its inhabitants and in affluence of all kinds.'

When news of the very existence of such a city reached peoples whose well-being depended, to no small extent, on plunder, their curiosity was naturally aroused, as was their cupidity. If ever they had an opportunity of attacking it they would clearly do so, and it became one of the principal concerns of Constantine and his more enlightened successors to make the defences of the city as nearly impregnable as possible.

Its splendour, its wealth and its military defences apart, Constantinople had one other source of strength. This was the power of faith.

When Constantine began the building of New Rome, the population of the Empire as a whole was thought to have been about one-fifth Christian.[3] The gospel had been accepted much more readily among the Greek-speaking peoples of the East and in Asia Minor than in western Europe.

By the year 300 more than half the population of Egypt was probably Christian, and there were flourishing churches based in Antioch, Caesarea and Tyre. At the same period, of the million or more inhabitants of Rome, probably no more than sixty or seventy thousand were Christians.[4] Intellectually too the churchmen in the East were far more distinguished, and they had a tendency to despise the simplicity and ignorance of their western counterparts.

Persecution of Christians continued until the beginning of the fourth century, largely according to the whims of individual emperors. Diocletian was among the persecutors. Constantine gave the Christian Church not only freedom to practise, but a temporal authority such as it had never known before. He himself was a convert, persuaded, as he explained to his biographer, Bishop Eusebius of Caesarea, by the sudden spectacle of a 'cross of light in the sky' and by his success in battle which followed. From that moment he continued what a latter-day historian has described as 'his determined but rather confused transition from Sun-worship to the Christian faith.'[5]

Characteristically he instituted the building of a wealth of splendid churches in Constantinople and instructed Eusebius to provide them with fifty beautifully written and bound copies of the Bible. He endowed the Church with large estates and exempted the clergy from taxes. One Greek city even petitioned him for exemption from taxation on the grounds that all its citizens had become Christian.

Constantine also accorded the Church new judicial rights when he decreed that before the final judgement in any law-suit either party might transfer the case to the jurisdiction of the local bishop.[6] Nevertheless, when a council of 220 bishops, nearly all of them Greek-speaking, assembled at Nicaea in Asia Minor in 325 to give judgement on doctrine, it was Constantine who presided and led the discussions.

Under Constantine the Church acquired spiritual authority, temporal powers, wealth and respect such as it had never known before. Late in the tenth century emissaries sent by the Prince of Kiev to Byzantium were to say on their return: 'We do not know whether we were in heaven or on earth, and we cannot describe it. We only know that God dwells there among men.' The origins of the wonders they witnessed were to be found in the New Rome which Constantine created.

CHAPTER 9

THE COURT OF THEODOSIUS II

By the mid fifth century, when the main threat to its peace was posed by Attila, the New Rome which Constantine had founded had undergone political and other changes. It had also been greatly strengthened against possible attack by land.

Some of Constantine's policies were soon put into reverse by his successors. His kinsman, the Emperor Julian, an earnest, well-read, somewhat prickly character, not unlike certain determined latter-day humanists, became known to posterity as Julian the Apostate.

Brought up as a Christian and guided by Constantine's biographer, Bishop Eusebius, he spent more than six years as a student, during which time he became increasingly attracted by Hellenistic culture and the ancient pagan faiths.

His intentions were of the best. On becoming Emperor he issued an edict of universal tolerance and tried to restore the ancient faiths through the influence of schools, but his success was limited. A Christian who had been a contemporary of his as a student wrote of his 'wild, darting eye, haughty way of breathing down a prominent nose and nervous and uncontrolled laughter.'[1]

On becoming Emperor he dismissed the bulk of the large domestic staff which his predecessor, Constantius II, had accumulated, and instituted a programme of austerity. He also wrote a hymn seventeen thousand words in length, and supposedly composed in a single night, to a pagan goddess, asking her to 'grant to the Roman people that they cleanse themselves of the stain of impiety.'

Constantius II had received an ultimatum from King Shapur of Persia, stating as his minimum demand the cession of Armenia and

Mesopotamia. This was resisted, but Persian armies occupied considerable territory in Asia Minor, and, after becoming Emperor, Julian decided to send a force to attack them.

With more courage than judgement he led it into battle without troubling to strap on his breastplate. He was struck by a spear and died of his wounds. The captain of his bodyguard, Jovian, who became Emperor for a year, accepted the terms of a treaty yielding five frontier provinces, which Diocletian had captured, to the Persians.[2]

It was not until the reign of Theodosius I, who became Emperor in 379, that Constantine's policies were generally implemented or developed. Ecclesiastical historians were to apply to him, as they did to Constantine, the attribute 'the Great'.

Theodosius was the first of the emperors to make Constantinople his permanent residence. For all his pride in his new creation, Constantine spent much of his time outside it. It was in a suburb of Nicomedia, Diocletian's old capital, that he died. Jovian never reached Constantinople, and other emperors maintained the peripatetic lifestyle of so many of their predecessors.

Constantine had believed in a united Church under central control, but he had been generally tolerant of paganism. Theodosius considered stronger measures were needed and issued a decree in 397 prohibiting pagan worship.

He also commanded his subjects to accept as the orthodox faith the doctrines propounded at the Council of Nicaea, over which Constantine had presided. He then transferred all the Arian churches in Constantinople to the control of the Orthodox and prohibited heretics from worshipping in public.

Theodosius's religious policy, like that of Constantine, clearly derived from deep conviction, as he showed when, unlike any Roman Emperor before him, he went bare-headed, and dressed in sackcloth, to the cathedral in Milan to beg forgiveness for his sins. This he had been instructed to do by Bishop Ambrose, a man of commanding intellect.

Constantine had added greatly to the efficiency of the imperial armies by creating a striking force that could be marched without delay to any threatened area. He had also increased the army's manpower by a steady enrolment of Germans. Theodosius went even further.

After the military disaster suffered by the Emperor Valens at the hands of Goths who had been accepted as settlers within the Empire, the problem of how to absorb these people successfully had remained. Theodosius largely solved it by a diplomatic triumph following some two years of negotiations.

The essence of his plan was the enrolment of large numbers of Goths in the legions. They were offered high rates of pay and exemption from taxes, and a considerable degree of autonomy was granted to the settlers. The effect was to create new and powerful forces which could be used to resist Persians, Huns and others who threatened the Empire.

The settlement was moreover achieved without creating new internal dangers to the Empire in the East through the presence of large numbers of well-armed foreigners. In this respect the Empire in the West was to be less fortunate.

Agreement was reached too in a spirit of considerable good-will. The ageing Goth ruler Athanaric, who had been forced by the Huns to take refuge in Transylvania, was formally invited to Constantinople, Theodosius meeting him outside the walls and conducting him to his palace.

On seeing the wonders of Constantinople, Athanaric, according to Jordanes, declared: 'Now do I at last behold what I had often heard and deemed incredible.' Theodosius's court orator stated: 'Rome's most courageous enemies will become her truest and most loyal friends.'[3]

In addition to all this Theodosius agreed peace terms with the Persian Empire which ensured stability for many years.

The Emperor in the East when Attila became King of the Huns was Theodosius I's grandson, who was also named Theodosius. Whereas Theodosius I came to power as an experienced campaigner in Britain and the Balkans, his grandson, somewhat unusually, succeeded his father Arcadius at the age of seven.

While he remained a child the two most powerful figures in Constantinople were the prefect Anthemius and Theodosius's eldest sister, Pulcheria, who in 414, when the Emperor was fourteen, formally became his guardian. She herself was only sixteen.

Pulcheria was a formidable woman. Early in life she decided to dedicate herself to perpetual virginity, and, used as she already was to exercising authority, she persuaded her two sisters to follow her example. In the words of Gibbon, 'their palace was converted into a monastery, and all males – except the guides of their conscience, the saints who had forgotten the distinction of sexes – were scrupulously excluded from the holy threshold.'

He went on: 'Pulcheria, her two sisters, and a chosen train of favourite damsels, formed a religious community: they renounced the vanity of dress, interrupted by frequent fasts their simple and frugal diet, allotted a portion of their time to works of embroidery, and devoted several hours of the day and night to the exercises of prayer and psalmody.'

While living in this relative seclusion, Pulcheria found time to pay for the building of numerous splendid churches in different parts of the Empire in the East. She also kept a close watch over the conduct of her brother and even decided who should be his wife.

Surprisingly, it may be thought, she chose a girl of exceptional beauty named Athenais, who was the daughter of a university professor. Pulcheria was said to have been favourably impressed by the way in which the girl spoke Greek.

Theodosius not only approved of his sister's choice, but he seems to have fallen in love with Athenais. When she presented him with a daughter he raised her to the rank of Augusta with her new name of Eudocia, and the influence of Pulcheria began to decline.

The new Empress, who in addition to her beauty had inherited much of her father's talent, increasingly replaced Pulcheria as a powerful influence at court. The creation of a great new centre of learning in the University of Constantinople was attributable in part to this. In her later years Eudocia retired to Jerusalem, where she wrote commentaries on different Old Testament books and poems on her husband's achievements.

Theodosius grew up in an atmosphere in which religious opinions were advanced with force and authority and repudiated no less strenuously. Constantine and Theodosius I had sought orthodoxy in belief and centralization of spiritual power, but they could not prevent theological debate, nor the vituperation that frequently accompanied it.

There were recorded instances of beards being pulled and Bibles being hurled, and Jordanes described the prevailing atmosphere in

Constantinople convincingly when he wrote: 'The city is full of mechanics, who are all of them profound theologians and preach in the shops and the streets. If you desire a man to change a piece of silver he informs you where the Son differs from the Father.'

Among the most vigorous advocates of his own interpretation of the true faith was St John Chrysostom, also known as John of Antioch, who was appointed Bishop of Constantinople after spending ten years living a life of asceticism in the desert. He made himself unpopular in a number of quarters by prohibiting priests from employing lay sisters as servants and confining monks whom he considered under-employed to monasteries.

St John and the Empress Eudocia fought a spiritual running battle, knowledge of which became public from time to time, as when, from the pulpit, he likened her to Herodias demanding the head of John the Baptist. Popular support for the Bishop tended to grow when attempts by the Empress to have him ousted were followed by fires and earthquakes, which in turn led to her having miscarriages.

St John Chrysostom recorded his own impressions of the Emperor who grew up in these circumstances. 'Because he was shut up in the palace,' he wrote, 'he did not grow to any size.' He added: 'His forbearance and friendliness conquered all men. He enjoyed the syllogisms of Aristotle, practised his philosophy in action, and wholly put aside anger, violence, grief, pleasure and bloodshed.'

This was probably a fair judgement. Theodosius was well read, particularly in the Scriptures. He fasted regularly. He disliked capital punishment and frequently pardoned those who had been condemned to death. He also insisted that prisoners should be taken to a bath-house every Sunday.[4]

It is an attractive character which emerges. It is also unlike those of most of the politically minded soldiers who constituted so many of his predecessors. As such it may be thought the character of a man little suited to cope with the new kind of menace presented by Attila and his Huns.

In addition to the powerful influences of women and priests, Theodosius had another adviser on whom he came to rely. This was a eunuch named Chrysaphius.

The position of grand chamberlain, nearly always a eunuch, who exercised general authority over court officials and over imperial finances, had not yet been firmly established in the Empire in the East. Chrysaphius was a forerunner of many to come, some of them able administrators, all of them envied for the power they exercised.

Chrysaphius was to play an important and sinister role in the relations between Theodosius and Attila. Of him a contemporary wrote that 'he controlled everything, plundering the possessions of all and being hated by all.'[5]

Although Theodosius's own interests were not military, the defences of Constantinople were in fact greatly strengthened during his reign. The credit for this lay, not with the Emperor, who was a child when the work began, but with the Praetorian Prefect Anthemius.

Anthemius decided that the walls that Constantine had built gave inadequate protection, and he instituted a new defensive system. The most important feature of this was a main or inner wall more than four metres thick and topped by ninety-six towers. These towers were nearly twenty metres high and were placed at intervals of about sixty metres.

An outer wall also had ninety-six towers, and there was a terraced area between the two walls about twenty metres broad. The walls were built predominantly of stone, though with here and there a mixture of stone and brick. There were ten gates, five of which were used exclusively for military purposes. The most famous was the Golden Gate facing the Sea of Marmora.[6]

The walls would be added to later, but the system devised by Anthemius was essentially that which enabled the city of Constantinople to remain unconquered for a thousand years.

CHAPTER 10

A PLOT TO MURDER ATTILA

Among those who knew Chrysaphius well was the distinguished author, Priscus of Panium. Priscus wrote in Greek and as a historian was clearly influenced by the great Greek descriptive writers, Herodotus and Xenophon. He was also, like Thucydides, a reporter of current events in which he participated.

Priscus's *History of Byzantium* filled seven volumes. Unfortunately the greater part has been lost. What remains includes by far the most convincing first-hand account of the clash of personalities and interests between Attila and the regime of Theodosius II.

Priscus was an admirer of an earlier wielded of great power in Constantinople named Cyrus, whom he described as 'a pagan, a poet and a friend of the Empress Eudoxia.' Cyrus was considered incorruptible and was so popular that the factions at the chariot races in the hippodrome shouted his name with enthusiasm.

Theodosius's reaction to this had been to relieve him of his post, deprive him of his property and, somewhat curiously, to appoint him Bishop of Smyrna. Chrysaphius, his successor, was in almost every respect his opposite, being, in Priscus's opinion, corrupt, power-hungry and widely hated.

The mission sent by Attila to Constantinople in which he demanded major territorial changes was headed by the Skirian king, Edika, and by Orestes, the father of the future Roman Emperor. At one of their meetings with Chrysaphius, Edika, through an interpreter named Bigilas, expressed his astonishment at the splendour of the royal apartments.

Chrysaphius, according to Priscus, said that Edika might also be 'the lord of a golden-roofed house and of such wealth if he would disregard

Scythian matters and take up Roman ways.' Edika replied quite properly that 'it was not right for the servant of another master to do this without his lord's permission.'

Chrysaphius then asked Edika whether he had easy access to Attila's presence and how much influence he wielded. Edika said that he was an intimate friend of Attila and that he was entrusted with his bodyguard along with men chosen for this duty. On specified days each of them in turn guarded Attila with arms.

This interested Chrysaphius greatly, and he invited Edika to dinner, saying that he must make sure not to bring Orestes or any of the other envoys with him.

The dinner took place in Chrysaphius's home. Bigilas, who, as a Hunnic-speaker in the imperial service, had a somewhat ambivalent position, was present as interpreter. Chrysaphius told Edika he had a proposition to make and swore Edika to secrecy. Edika undertook not to reveal whatever Chrysaphius told him even if he did not agree to carry out his suggestions.

'Then the eunuch said to Edika that if, having crossed into Scythia, he should slay Attila and come back to the Romans, he would have a happy life and great wealth. Edika promised and said that he needed money for the deed, not a great deal, but fifty pounds of gold to be given to the force under his command so that they might perfectly cooperate with him in the attack.'

Edika was aware that he might have to explain to Attila how the fifty pounds of gold had been come by, and for what purpose it was to be used. To overcome this difficulty the two conspirators decided to trust Bigilas and to use him as a go-between, who could bring a message explaining how and where the gold should be delivered.

Chrysaphius's next move was to inform the Emperor Theodosius of his plan. He in turn consulted his Master of Offices, Martialus, who controlled all the messengers, interpreters and soldiers of the imperial bodyguard. The upshot of their discussions was a decision to appoint a man of proved integrity and distinction to head an embassy to Attila's court.

He would be told nothing of the murder plot, and Bigilas would be a relatively junior member of the mission. The practice, widespread in the twentieth century, of giving diplomatic cover to would-be assassins, of whose duties the ambassador was kept in ignorance, had well-established precedents.

Theodosius's choice as ambassador was Maximinus, who had played an important part in negotiating a treaty with the Persians more than a quarter of a century earlier. He had performed admirably in the past as a soldier no less than as a diplomat, and was noted for his eloquence.

Maximinus thereupon invited Priscus to accompany him on the mission. There were plenty of precedents for appointing an accomplished man of letters as a member of a mission on a long journey to a country where the cultural amenities were likely to be few. Pliny the Younger was among those who had filled such a role. 'Maximinus', Priscus wrote, 'by his entreaties persuaded me to set out on the embassy with him.'

To Maximinus and to Priscus one of the main purposes of the embassy was represented as being the settlement of the matrimonial problems of Attila's secretary, Constantius. He had been promised a rich and noble wife from the court of Constantinople. The girl first chosen had expressed her reluctance, and her family's fortune had then been confiscated. Constantius had therefore looked further and had been promised a widow of exceptional beauty and wealth.

Attila stated that he would be willing to come as far as Sofia (Sardica) to meet the mission provided its members were sufficiently high-ranking, and after some show of reluctance the Emperor agreed.

The mission, under the leadership of Maximinus, set out early in the summer of 449. Edika, Orestes and Bigilas were among the travelling group. So were a number of Huns, whom Priscus did not name and who were evidently under Edika's orders. There were also seventeen Hun fugitives whose return Attila had demanded.

The journey from Constantinople to Sofia took thirteen days, and at the end of it Maximinus felt it incumbent on him to entertain Edika and Orestes and their principal followers to dinner. Sofia was a ruined and deserted city, but some sheep and cattle were obtained and duly slaughtered.

The dinner was not altogether a success. The Huns toasted the health of Attila, and Maximinus that of Theodosius. Bigilas, possibly under the influence of drink, then made the tactless remark that it was improper to mention the name of a god such as Theodosius in the same breath as that of a mere man such as Attila.

In the words of Priscus, 'the Huns were irritated and, growing hot, little by little became angry. But we turned the talk to other matters, and with friendly overtures they themselves calmed down their spirit.' But Bigilas's words were not forgotten.

As a further goodwill gesture Maximinus presented both Edika and Orestes with some Indian pearls and some silks, but after the dinner Orestes, having waited until Edika had left, made an observation that puzzled both Maximinus and Priscus. He congratulated Maximinus on his cleverness in not following the example of some court officials by inviting Edika to dine with him alone.

'On the next day,' Priscus wrote, 'as we were advancing we told Bigilas what Orestes had said to us. He said that Orestes ought not to be angry that he had not had the same treatment as Edika, for he was a servant and secretary of Attila, but Edika was a man foremost in military matters and, since he was of the Hunnish race, far superior to Orestes.'

Apart from the fact that Edika was not a Hun it was a skilfully contrived explanation. Neither Maximinus nor Priscus yet knew the underlying meaning of what Orestes had said at the end of the dinner, but there can be little doubt that Bigilas did.

Attila did not come to Sofia, and it was some time before the mission was allowed to make direct contact with him. The mission therefore continued to Nish, which, some six years after its destruction, was still a scene of desolation.

The splendid buildings with which the Emperor Constantine had embellished the city of his birth were irreparably lost. The able-bodied who had survived the sacking of the city had all fled, leaving only the sick behind. A halt was made near a river, and Priscus observed that 'every place on the bank was full of the bones of those slain in the war.'

After some hard going in hilly terrain in Serbia, where they had found navigation difficult, the members of the mission reached the Danube. There, Priscus wrote, 'barbarian ferrymen received us, and in single-log boats, which they themselves build, cutting and hollowing out the trees, they ferried us across the Danube river.'

News was received that Attila was intending to enter imperial territory for the purpose of hunting, but this was treated with scepticism, some members of the mission believing that it might be the prelude to launching another military campaign.

Before long it became evident that for the mission to come into the presence of Attila would not be easy. Edika with some of his followers went ahead as herald to announce the mission's arrival, and in response two Hun horsemen appeared and directed the remainder of the mission towards Attila's tents.

Maximinus decided to pitch the mission's own tents on a hill, but was told that this would not be allowed, as Attila's tents were on lower ground. Edika then returned with Orestes and Scotta and surprised Maximinus and Priscus by enquiring what they intended to achieve by their embassy. Bigilas showed signs of anxiety, evidently suspecting Edika of having betrayed their secret plan to Attila.

Maximinus insisted on the embassy's right of direct access to Attila, and this seemed to have some effect. Then, in Priscus's words, 'our baggage had already been packed on the beasts of burden, and, having no choice, we were trying to begin our journey during the night when other barbarians came and said that Attila bade us wait on account of the hour. At the very place from which we had just set out some men arrived, bringing us an ox and river fish from Attila, and so we dined and then turned to sleep.'

Not long afterwards Maximinus, Priscus and others were summoned to Attila's tent. There they found him seated on a wooden stool. After a brief exchange of courtesies Attila turned on Bigilas and demanded how he dared come into his presence when he knew that the terms agreed with Anatolius for the return of Hun fugitives had not been fulfilled.

Bigilas attempted to explain that they had been – Maximinus's mission had already handed over some of the Huns who had travelled with it – but, in Priscus's words, 'Attila became even angrier and, railing at him violently, said with a shout that he would have impaled him and given him to the birds for food if he had not thought it an outrage to the law of embassies.'

After the meeting Bigilas was clearly chastened and expressed his surprise to Priscus that Attila had spoken to him as he had done. Priscus, who, like Maximinus, still knew nothing of the murder plot, replied in all innocence that Attila might have learned of Bigilas's injudicious comparison between Attila the man and Theodosius the god.

Edika then took Bigilas aside and, as Priscus later learned, told him the time had come for the gold to be made available to those who would take part in the assassination. When Priscus asked what their discussion had been about, Bigilas became evasive. The next day Bigilas left, ostensibly to look into the question of the return of Hun fugitives, and the mission continued its journey northward.

Priscus was impressed by the hospitality the mission received as it travelled. Food was supplied generously, as was mead. When the mission's tents were blown over in a heavy storm, 'the barbarians', he wrote, 'summoned us to their own huts and, burning a great many reeds, furnished us shelter.'

The village where this happened was ruled by a woman, who, it emerged, was one of Bleda's former wives. She did not only send food. She also provided 'good-looking women to comfort us.' Describing this as 'a Scythian compliment', Priscus added: 'We showed them kindness but refused intercourse with them.' In return for the hospitality they had received the mission presented Bleda's widow with three silver goblets, furs, pepper from India and dates.

The mission travelled for another week and was then told by its guides that it must halt for a time. Attila, it was explained, was travelling along the same route and the mission must arrive at its destination after he did.

Attila's entrance into a village was a colourful affair. A select band of women came out to meet him and then marched ahead of him in separate files. The gaps between the files were filled by white linen veils, which the women carried above their heads and which served as a canopy for a chorus of young girls, who sang laudatory hymns.

As they neared the site of Attila's court in the region of the river Tisza, the members of the mission found themselves more and more in contact with men from the Western Roman Empire, and they were impressed by these men's standing and calibre. Among them was Orestes' father-in-law, Romanus, the commander of the military forces in Noricum.

Finally the mission reached its destination. Maximinus and Priscus were sitting in their tent when Orestes' father, a Roman named Tatulus, entered and said: 'Attila invites you both to a banquet.' The time fixed was 'about the ninth hour of the day' – that is to say three o'clock in the afternoon.

CHAPTER 11

THE MURDER PLOT DISCOVERED

The first banquet to which Maximinus and Priscus were invited by Attila was attended by some of the Western Romans whom they had already met and who, they discovered, were also part of an embassy to Attila. Of the banquet Priscus wrote: 'We stood on the threshold before Attila. The cup-bearers gave us a cup, according to local custom, so that we might pray before sitting down. When this was done and we had tasted the cup we went to the seats in which we were to sit while dining.

'All the chairs were ranged along the walls of the house on either side. In the middle sat Attila on a couch, another couch being set behind him. At the back of this steps led up to his bed, which was covered with white linens and coloured embroideries for ornament, just as the Hellenes and Romans prepare for those who marry.'

The seating arrangements gave Priscus an opportunity to gauge the relative importance of the principal guests. 'The position of those dining on the right of Attila', he wrote, 'is considered the most honourable, and second the position on the left, where we happened to be.' The chair immediately to the right of Attila's couch was occupied by Onegesius, the Hellenized foreigner, who was the chamberlain or master of Attila's household. Opposite Onegesius were two of Attila's sons.

Wine was brought and salutations made according to strict rules of decorum. Attila's own servant was the first to bring in food, and other servants followed with provisions for the guests. All this was fairly predictable, but Priscus then made a discovery that interested him.

'While sumptuous food, served on silver plates,' he wrote, 'had been prepared for the other barbarians and for us, for Attila there was nothing but meat on a wooden platter. He showed himself temperate in all other ways too, for gold and silver goblets were offered to the men at the feast, but his mug was of wood.'

In dress and general appearance also Attila was noticeably different from the others present. 'His dress was plain, having care for nothing other than to be clean, nor was the sword by his side, nor the clasps of his barbarian boots, nor the bridle of his horse, like those of the Scythians, adorned with gold or gems or anything of high price.'

The singing, which followed the banqueting, excited some of the guests with memories of Attila's victories in war. Others were moved to tears. Various entertainments were then provided, one of which made Priscus aware of the difference of opinion between Attila and Bleda, to which some had attached importance. This was the performance of Zerko, the dwarf.

Of the dwarf himself Priscus wrote: 'He was somewhat short, hump-shouldered, with distorted feet and a nose indicated only by the nostrils because of its exceeding flatness.' As an entertainer he was clearly a success. 'By his appearance, his dress, his voice and the words he confusedly uttered – for he mixed the tongue of the Huns and the Goths with that of the Latins – he softened everyone except Attila and caused unquenchable laughter to arise.'

Attila, Priscus noted, 'remained unmoved.' Perhaps his difference with Bleda in this matter was simply one of taste.

Priscus observed that Attila did not show his feelings readily. 'Neither in speech nor action did he reveal that he had any laughter in him except when his youngest son – Ernak was the boy's name – came in and stood before him. He pinched the boy's cheeks and looked on him with serene laughter.'

The reason given to Priscus by one of the other diners for Attila's evident preference for his youngest son was a prophecy by a soothsayer that Attila's 'race would fail but would be restored by this son.' As an explanation it was plausible, but not necessarily correct.

Maximinus and Priscus were entertained by Attila to more than one banquet, and Priscus was impressed by the unfailing courtesy he showed them. They were also received quite separately by Attila's principal wife, Kreka, who had borne him three sons.

Her quarters, Priscus observed, included 'numerous buildings, some of carved boards beautifully fitted together, others fastened on round wooden blocks, which rose to a moderate height from the ground.' He went on: 'Having been admitted by the barbarians at the door, I found her reclining on a couch. The floor of the room was covered with woollen mats for walking on. A number of servants stood round her, and maids sitting on the floor in front of her embroidered with colours linen cloths intended to be placed over the Scythian dress for ornament.'

There were other revealing encounters and spectacles. Of Attila's palace Priscus wrote: 'Though of wood, like all the better buildings of the city, it contains, nevertheless, baths of stone and marble like those of Rome. The stone was transported from Pannonia, for there are no quarries in this part of the world.'

The builder of the baths was a Greek architect, who had been captured in Mitrovica. He had hoped to win his freedom by the work he had done, but found himself obliged to keep the baths in running order. 'As they are something of a marvel to the Huns,' Priscus wrote, 'the chances are that this will be a job for life.'

It was possible for freedom to be obtained by services rendered, as Priscus learned from a man who clearly interested him greatly. The man, he wrote, 'resembled a well-to-do Hun, having his hair cut in a circle after the Hun fashion. Having returned his salutation, I found myself quizzing him as to his antecedents. To justify my curiosity I explained that it was prompted by the purity of his Hellenic accent.'

Priscus went on: 'This earned a smile and the admission that he was a Greek by birth, a Hellene who had gone as a merchant to Viminiacum [Kostolac] on the Danube. There he had settled and married a very rich wife. But the city fell prey to the Huns, and he was stripped of his wealth. He had accepted his fate philosophically, served his master faithfully, and fought under him in expeditions against the Romans. With the spoils of war he had been able to obtain his freedom.'

What followed shed a revealing light on how life could be lived under Attila's rule.

'He was now married to a Hun,' Priscus wrote, 'and he offered the highest possible tribute to primitive society by insisting that he was far better off among the Huns than he had been under us Romans. He gave me an astonishing picture of the happy and care-free existence he led among these barbarians. "It is," he said, "the simple life, the wholesome life a man has the right to expect, secure from injustice, exactions, insults from the powerful, the burden of taxation, the delays and corruption of law courts."'

Priscus also had convincing evidence of the loyalty Attila's principal officials felt towards him. Maximinus suggested it might be advantageous for Onegesius to visit the Emperor in Constantinople and 'by his wisdom arrange the objects of dispute between the Romans and Huns.'

Onegesius evidently thought Maximinus was setting a trap for him and trying to suborn him. In Priscus's words, 'Onegesius said he would inform the Emperor and his ministers of Attila's wishes, but the Romans need not think they could ever prevail with him to betray his master or neglect his Scythian training and his wives and children, nor to prefer wealth among the Romans to bondage with Attila.'

The climax of the mission to Attila came when Bigilas returned. He was led into Attila's presence and asked to explain why he carried so much gold. Bigilas had his story prepared. 'He answered', Priscus wrote, 'that it was for provisioning himself and those accompanying him so that, through lack of supplies or scarcity of horses or baggage animals expended on the long journey, he might not stray from his zeal for the embassy.'

As an additional justification he added that the gold 'was also supplied to purchase fugitives, for many in Roman territory had begged him to liberate their kinsmen.'

Attila knew the truth. Indeed, he had known it for some time. 'No longer, you worthless beast,' he said, 'will you escape justice by deception. Nor will there be any excuse sufficient for you to avoid punishment.'

On his return journey Bigilas had been accompanied by his son. Attila now threatened to have the son struck down by a sword unless Bigilas told him the whole truth.

'When he beheld his son under threat of death,' Priscus wrote, 'he took to tears and lamentations and called aloud on justice to turn the sword against himself and not against a youth who had done no wrong. With no hesitation he told of the plans made by himself, Edika, the eunuch and the Emperor, and begged unceasingly to be put to death and his son set free.'

Priscus was convinced that Attila had learned of the plot to murder him from Edika. Whether Edika had never intended to kill Attila, or whether he had initially fallen for Chrysaphius's plan and then, having become aware of Orestes' suspicions, had changed his mind, is debatable.

Attila evidently gave him the benefit of any doubt he may have had. As for Bigilas, he ordered that he should be kept in chains until his son had returned from Constantinople with a further fifty pounds in gold by way of ransom money.

This the son did, and Attila's final decision was that Orestes should return to Constantinople with Bigilas, and that Bigilas should be obliged to wear a bag around his neck containing a hundred pounds in gold. In this condition he was to be brought into the presence of Theodosius as a reminder of the part the Emperor had played in the plot to murder Attila.

As a verdict it was generous, even magnanimous, in that it spared the life of a man who had intended to kill Attila for a pecuniary reward. It was also magnificently scornful of the connivance in the whole sordid affair of the man who was heir to the greatest empire on earth.

Priscus was a highly civilized man and an acute observer, who formed his own impressions and opinions. But he also had some of the prejudices common among people of his standing. As a Greek-speaking Roman citizen he referred to Huns, Goths and other foreigners, whom he encountered, almost indiscriminately as 'barbarians' or 'Scythians'.

He did not find Attila's appearance congenial or attractive. The short, square body, the large head, the deep-seated eyes, the swarthy complexion, the flat nose and the few sparse hairs in place of a beard did not represent, to a man like Priscus, masculine good looks.

Yet the more he observed Attila the more he seems to have been impressed by him. Attila's abstemiousness, where there was plenty, and his preference for plain rather than gaudy or luxurious clothing seemed to Priscus to be marks of distinction. The standard of living he enjoyed was no doubt higher than Priscus had expected, and he evidently assumed it to be his right.

He showed himself to be a loving father with a wife who was accorded a position of dignity. His close associates were fiercely loyal to him, and at least one man in a lowlier position could not speak too highly of the nature of the society he ruled.

He was courteous to ambassadors and aware of the niceties of diplomacy, while making it clear that he could regard only the ambassador's master as in any way his equal. He was a big enough man to be magnanimous in victory, even over a venal and cringing would-be assassin.

Summarizing his impressions, Priscus wrote that Attila was 'a man born to shake the races of the world. The proud man's power was to be seen in the very movements of his body.'

It was the verdict of the only human being to meet Attila and speak with him who has left any surviving written record. As such it is the closest witness we have to the truth.

CHAPTER 12

THE WEAKNESS OF THE WEST

The immediate achievements of Maximinus's mission were slight. The problem of finding a suitable bride for Attila's secretary, Constantius, was duly solved, but that of the fugitive Huns was much more intractable.

Valuable insight was, however, gained into Attila's manner of conducting business, and much was learnt about his strength as a ruler in his own kingdom. The mission also returned with at least one interesting piece of military intelligence.

In a conversation Maximinus and Priscus had with Romulus, the military governor of Noricum, they learned that, in his opinion, no one else had achieved so much in so short a time as Attila had done, and that his next move might well be to attack Persia. Huns had earlier reached Persian territory, and Romulus did not think Attila would have much difficulty in doing the same.

There were other West Romans present at the discussion. Some considered that such a move would provide a welcome respite to the Roman Empire, but one man named Constantiolus said that if the Persian Empire collapsed, as well it might after a Hun invasion, the Roman Empire would probably be the next victim.[1]

In negotiations that followed Maximinus's mission, Attila showed himself remarkably amenable to suggestions put forward by the government in Constantinople. He agreed to release large numbers of Roman prisoners without ransom. He withdrew the demand he had made, not unreasonably, for Chrysaphius to be put to death for his part in the murder plot, and he even abandoned his requirement for a large stretch of territory to the north of Nish to be ceded.[2]

The explanation of Attila's change of policy was, no doubt, that he was already directing his attention to other lands, and for this purpose he wanted stability and peace in his relations with the Eastern Empire.

Then, in 450, the year after Maximinus's mission had been sent to Attila, an event occurred which was to have important consequences for the relations between the Eastern Empire and the Huns. On 28 July, when out riding, the Emperor Theodosius II fell from his horse. He died soon afterwards from his injuries.

Power was promptly seized by Pulcheria, who, at a fairly advanced age, entered into a form of marriage with the man who, she had decided, was to be the next Emperor. Marcian, who was aged about sixty when he succeeded, was an experienced general. He had known real poverty when young and had achieved success by campaigning in Persia and Africa. The quality that seems to have appealed most strongly to Pulcheria was his piety.[3]

The change of ruler brought the end of Chrysaphius's long exercise of power, and he was publicly executed without trial. Another change which Marcian's regime introduced was a decision to withhold the annual subsidies in gold which were being paid to the Huns. This was part of a general reform of finances.

Attila did not immediately respond to the change, for he was no longer primarily interested in the Empire in the East.

To assess the magnitude of the task confronting Attila when he decided to turn his attention to the West, it is necessary to consider what had happened in the preceding half-century.

Theodosius I, who died in 395, had been a unifying force within the Empire, both East and West benefiting from his diligence and concern with administrative detail. He accepted Diocletian's doctrine that there should be two emperors, but he himself was active politically, militarily and in Church matters, both in East and West. When a vacancy for a new emperor occurred he made it clear that it was his business to decide who was to fill it.

The arrangements he made for his succession, by contrast, accentuated and, in the outcome, perpetuated the division between the two parts of the Empire. The eastern part he left to his elder son, Arcadius, who was seventeen when Theodosius died. His younger son, Honorius, inherited the western part at the age of ten.

Neither son had more than a fraction of the ability of their father. Arcadius, to the public advantage, died young and was succeeded by Theodosius II.

Honorius, unfortunately for the Western Empire, lived longer, and during his reign weaknesses became apparent in the West, from which the East was largely immune. These weaknesses were increasingly brought to the attention of Attila by the advisers who surrounded him and by the ambassadors who visited him from the West.

There were a number of reasons why in the first half of the fifth century the Western Empire became more vulnerable to attack than the Eastern. One was the strength of the walls of Constantinople. Another was the difference in the parts played by Germanic peoples who had settled within the imperial boundaries.

During the reign of Honorius, military policy was largely dictated by Flavius Stilicho, who was the son of a Vandal. Stilicho had attracted the attention of Theodosius I, who, after sending him on an embassy to Persia, appointed him military commander in Thrace. He then went even further and arranged Stilicho's marriage to his own niece and adopted daughter, Serena. After Theodosius's death, Stilicho became Honorius's guardian and later, in effect, his prime minister.

Stilicho was a man of strikingly good looks and of broad culture. He became, possibly under the influence of his wife Serena, the patron of Claudian, the leading poet of their time, who responded by a series of panegyrics in verse. But, while he had his admirers, he also had his detractors, some of whom regarded him as a Vandal rather than a true Roman.

Stilicho was reviled for weakening the army and, in particular, for withdrawing the garrisons from the Rhine in order to have more troops at his disposal in Italy. In his defence it could be argued that he was confronted by steadily increasing costs in sustaining the defence of the Empire and by the reluctance of large numbers of Roman citizens, other than Germans, to undertake military service.

Increasingly Stilicho found himself reaching accommodation with peoples who might pose a military threat to the Empire. He began the practice, which Aetius was later to adopt, of getting military support from the barbarians in return for territorial concessions. He also made deals and compromises with a Germanic soldier, by the name of Alaric.

Alaric was a Visigoth who, like Stilicho, had been appointed to an important military post by Theodosius I, but was disappointed that he did not advance even further in the imperial service. He had a considerable following among the Goths in the Eastern Empire, and, in the words of Jordanes, he and they together decided 'rather to seek new kingdoms by their own labour than to slumber in peaceful subjection to the rule of others.'

The military force that Alaric assembled under his command approached Constantinople, but, finding that they could not break down the walls, he and his troops ranged widely through Greece much as Attila's forces were to do later. Then, in 400, Alaric took the decisive step of invading Italy, thereby obliging Stilicho to weaken the Empire's frontier defences.

The Visigoth advance into Italy was a migration no less than an invasion, for large numbers of women and children accompanied the army. This impaired its mobility, although other reasons were also advanced for a defeat it suffered at the hands of Stilicho's forces.

Alaric was a devout Arian Christian, an allegiance that was to influence his conduct and career on a number of occasions. He did not believe that Stilicho would attack on Easter Sunday. In this he was wrong. His army suffered the consequences of being taken by surprise, and in 402, or possibly 403, it withdrew from Italy.

Stilicho and Alaric later reached an agreement, and during the thirteen years in which Stilicho was the effective ruler of the Western Empire Alaric did not threaten it seriously. But Stilicho was still distrusted, and he was even suspected of conspiring with Alaric to have his own son proclaimed Emperor.

Stilicho's downfall came in 408. Having been obliged to take sanctuary in a church in Ravenna, he agreed to come out on being promised his freedom. The promise was ignored, and the Emperor Honorius feebly agreed to his execution.

In an upsurge of anti-immigrant feeling, large numbers of Goths serving in the Roman army were killed together with their wives and children. The natural consequence of this was that even larger numbers of fighting men transferred their allegiance to Alaric. A considerable number of them were Huns.

As a result Alaric was in a position to march on Rome as Hannibal had attempted to do nearly six centuries earlier. His forces reached the outskirts of the city in September 408, and there they remained as winter drew on.

As a siege it was extraordinarily successful. The city was soon short of food, and on being offered 5,000 pounds of gold, 20,000 pounds of silver, as well as silks, hides and pepper, Alaric agreed to withdraw.

In the two years following Stilicho's death the lack of judgement shown by Honorius and his advisers in dealing with Alaric was continual. Alaric, who had shown that he could conquer Rome if he wanted to, asked for territory to be made available as a permanent home for the Goths on the understanding that the territory would remain within the Empire, and that Alaric would ensure its defence.

The area he at first suggested included the site of present-day Venice and its hinterland, Slovenia and eastern Austria, but he later modified his demands, asking only for eastern Austria. Honorius turned down all proposals and even refused to grant Alaric a military title that he coveted, and which Stilicho had once held.

Alaric responded by besieging Rome again. This time he decided to appoint an alternative Emperor, a Greek named Attalus, and obtained the Senate's approval of his choice. Despite the power he now exercised he continued to regard himself as a subject of the Roman Empire, from whose ruler he wanted reasonable concessions. He openly declared himself to be 'the friend of peace and of the Romans.'[4]

Honorius had long been hoping for help from his nephew, Theodosius II, and when six legions arrived from the East to lend him support, he felt he could continue to defy Alaric.

Once again he made the wrong judgement. Alaric decided that Attalus served little useful purpose and removed him from office. In 410 he marched on Rome once more, and this time, instead of merely blockading the city until his demands were met, he ordered his army to enter and occupy it.

It did so with little difficulty, and what to many had been the unthinkable had happened. Rome was at the mercy of people whom its inhabitants had long been accustomed to despise and to dread and whom they called barbarians.

To Attila some four decades later one lesson was clear. Rome was far more vulnerable to an invading army than Constantinople. Its physical defences were far weaker, and its huge population could be starved before long into surrender.

During the forty years other factors had, however, affected the balance of power. One was the strength of feeling aroused by the occupation of Rome and the lessons learned from it. Another was the assumption of power by one of the ablest and most imaginative women of her age, indeed in the history of the Roman Empire. A third was the rise of a military commander whom Attila would have abundant reason to respect.

CHAPTER 13

THE EMPRESS IN RAVENNA

St Jerome expressed the feelings of many when he wrote of the occupation of Rome by Alaric's forces: 'Who will hereafter credit the fact, or what histories will seriously discuss it, that Rome has to fight within her own borders, not for glory, but for bare life; and that she does not even fight but buys the right to exist by giving gold and sacrificing all her substance?'

Much of the blame for what had happened he attributed to Stilicho. 'This humiliation', he wrote, 'has been brought upon her not by the fault of her Emperors, who are both most religious men, but by the crime of a half-barbarian traitor, who with our money has armed our foes against us.'

He wrote this in a letter to one of his female correspondents. Of her he asked: 'Dearest daughter in Christ, answer me this question: will you marry amid such scenes as these? Tell me, what kind of husband will you take? One that will run or one that will fight?'

A much more profound theologian than Jerome was also inspired to write at length by Alaric's occupation of Rome. He was St Augustine, the Bishop of Hippo (now Bona in Tunisia), whose massive work *The City of God* was, in part at least, a direct consequence of the extraordinary events that had taken place.

The most surprising aspect of the occupation of Rome was the forbearance that Alaric's troops showed. They remained in the city for only three days. Alaric, governed by his strong Christian convictions, issued orders that Church property was to be respected, and his orders were largely obeyed, even though many of the troops, the Huns in particular, were not themselves Christians.

In St Augustine's words, 'all the devastation, murder, spoliation, arson, cruelty that were inflicted during the recent disaster in Rome followed the usual custom of war. On the other hand there was much that followed a new fashion. The ferocity of the barbarians was so chastened that they even chose out and set aside basilicas filled to overflowing with people whose lives they spared. There no blow was struck, no person was snatched into slavery.'

The conclusion he drew was: 'This was due to the name of Christ and to the change-over to Christianity. Whoever cannot see that is blind.'[1]

Another observation St Augustine made concerned the Pope, Innocent I, who happened to be in Ravenna when Rome was occupied. On returning to Rome, Innocent found 'the great families gone and no one to rival him in rank or authority.'

In consequence, Augustine wrote, 'the triumph of Christianity and the greatness of the Papacy were both direct and immediate consequences of the fall of Rome.' Innocent, who, like Augustine, was canonized, did indeed greatly increase the authority of the Holy See. At the same time the temporal authority of Rome was even further diminished.

Alaric treated Rome barely as a stopping point. He evidently thought that the future of his followers, like that of the Vandals, should be in North Africa, which still served as a granary for Italy. He had advanced as far as Calabria when he contracted an illness and died suddenly.

A river was diverted from its course near Cosenza to allow a grave to be dug. Here Alaric was buried with some of his most precious treasures. When the work was completed the forced labourers who had carried it out were all killed to ensure that they could not reveal the site of the grave.

During his largely disastrous reign, which lasted twenty-eight years, Honorius, in addition to some useful legal reforms, could be credited with one important innovation. This was the establishment of a new capital of the Western Empire.

Following Diocletian's reforms, the capital had been moved from Rome to Milan. When Alaric's forces entered Italy, Honorius considered it prudent to abandon Milan and to choose as his capital a city that would be more easily defensible. His choice was Ravenna.

Like Constantinople, Ravenna depended for its defences, to a considerable extent, on water. The Emperor Augustus had fortified it with a system of canals, which linked it to the Po. He had also built a large harbour nearby, from which the Adriatic trade routes were largely controlled.[2]

'The city', Jordanes wrote, 'lies amid the streams of the Po between swamps and the sea, and is accessible only on one side. Situated in a corner of the Roman Empire above the Ionian Sea, it is hemmed in like an island by a flood of rushing waters.

'On the east it has the sea, and one who sails straight to it from the region of Corcyra and those parts of Hellas sweeps with his oars along the right hand coast, first touching Epirus, then Dalmatia, Liburnia and Istria and at last the Venetian Isles. But on the west it has swamps through which a sort of door has been left by a very narrow entrance. To the north is an arm of the Po, called the Fossa Asconis. On the south likewise is the Po itself, which they call the king of the rivers of Italy.'

When it was chosen as the capital, Ravenna lacked certain amenities. Another Gothic writer, Sidonius Apollinaris, wrote of it: 'With water all about us we could not quench our thirst. There was neither pure-flowing aqueduct, nor filterable cistern, nor trickling source, nor unclouded well. On the one side the salt tides assail the gates. On the other the movement of vessels stirs the filthy sediment in the canals, or the sluggish flow is fouled by the bargeman's poles, piercing the bottom of the slime.'

After that he let his fancy carry him away. 'On that marsh', he wrote, 'the laws of everything are always the wrong way about. The waters stand and the walls fall. The towers float and the ships stick fast. The sick man walks and the doctor lies abed. The baths are chill and the houses blaze. The clergy live by usury and the Syrian chants the psalms. Eunuchs take to arms and rough allies to letters.'[3]

As a city for good living Ravenna in the fifth century clearly had disadvantages. As an imperial capital from which invaders might be resisted its qualities were evident. For the exploitation of those qualities imaginative and determined leadership were needed. This was to be provided, not by Honorius, but by his sister, Galla Placidia.

Galla Placidia was in her early twenties, probably twenty-two, when Alaric's army captured Rome in 410. Unlike many prominent citizens she had not taken the opportunity of leaving the city before the assault began, and she was taken prisoner.

Before his final assault on Rome, Alaric had called upon his brother-in-law, Athaulf, who was operating in Pannonia, to bring him reinforcements, and these, consisting of Gothic and Hun troops, duly arrived. After Alaric's death Athaulf became the undisputed leader of the Goths in Italy.

Whether inspired by Placidia's beauty, as Jordanes suggested, or, as seems more probable, by the fact that she was an Emperor's sister, Athaulf decided that he would marry her. He therefore sent emissaries to Honorius with this proposal. Honorius rejected it scornfully, but Athaulf would not let Placidia go. Instead he took her with him on his next campaign.

Unlike Alaric, who had looked to North Africa for territory to be conquered and settled, Athaulf decided that his people should find a future in Gaul, and in 412 he led a large body of them over the Alps. He then followed Alaric's example by formally demanding from the Emperor a land where his people could settle.

Honorius was aware that the Roman hold over southern France was already tenuous, and he agreed to Athaulf's proposal. A large area of land in Aquitaine was ceded, and Athaulf and his followers established themselves in the cities of Bordeaux and Toulouse, thereby laying the foundations of the Visigoth Empire in southern France.

Honorius did make the suggestion that Athaulf should send back Placidia, but Athaulf had no intention of complying. The culmination of his triumph was a ceremony in Narbonne, at which he and Placidia were married. All the evidence suggests that Placidia was a willing bride and that this marriage of a Roman Emperor's daughter to a so-called barbarian king was happily accepted by both parties.

The anniversary of the marriage was celebrated in a spectacular manner. Placidia, in the garb of a Roman Empress, was seated on a throne, Athaulf having a subordinate position beside her. Fifty young men, each carrying two bowls, one filled with gold, the other with precious stones, presented them to Placidia. Attalus, who had briefly been

Alaric's puppet Emperor, was given the task of leading the singing.[4]

The marriage was brought to an abrupt end when Athaulf was murdered by one of his servants, named Sigeric, who celebrated his achievement by forcing Placidia, together with six children of Athaulf's by a former marriage, to walk in a procession through the streets for twelve miles in front of his horse.

Fortunately for Placidia, Sigeric was soon succeeded by a more enlightened ruler named Walia, who, realizing that she was a valuable property, allowed her to leave for Ravenna on payment of a substantial ransom, which took the form predominantly of wheat. She had by then spent some five years among the Goths, an experience that taught her much.

Placidia's second marriage seems to have been largely engineered by Honorius. His choice of a husband for her was Flavius Constantius, who had held the office of consul three times. Honorius also chose him as a co-emperor, although the appointment was not recognized by Theodosius II, who was now reigning in Constantinople.

Constantius died in 421, by which time Placidia had borne him a son and a daughter. Both were to play significant parts in the life of Attila and the relations between the Hun kingdom and the Roman Empire in the West.

After Constantius's death Placidia made her way to Constantinople, a journey whose outcome was to transform her life. It began in a hazardous manner. The ship in which she was sailing was struck by a gale and heavy seas, and, as a devout Christian, she made a vow to build a suitable church if she survived the crossing. She did, and the outcome was the church of San Giovanni Evangelista, which can be seen in Ravenna today.[5]

Once established in Constantinople, Placidia formed satisfactory relationships with Theodosius and his sisters. Honorius died in 423, and Placidia by then had sufficient influence to ensure that her six-year-old son was proclaimed Emperor in the West as Valentinian III.

Placidia became his guardian and regent. The woman who a few years earlier had been ignominiously dragged through the streets as a captive had become, and was to remain for a long time, the most powerful figure in the Western Empire.

CHAPTER 14

THE REVIVAL OF THE WESTERN EMPIRE

As a patroness of the Church and of the arts, Galla Placidia was both munificent and discriminating. The city of Ravenna bears abundant witness to this today. Her political achievements, though considerable, were more complex and diffuse.

Before her accession to power the Western Empire, after decades of misrule, had become vulnerable to attack from a variety of directions. Stilicho's withdrawal of frontier garrisons had opened floodgates. Alaric's occupation of Rome had proved the power of minority groups within the Empire.

During the period of Placidia's ascendancy the deterioration was largely reversed, and, contrary to the popular picture, which has prevailed for centuries, of an empire in steady decline, there were a number of military and diplomatic triumphs. These helped to shape the political scene at the time when Attila began to turn his attention to the West.

The most serious threat to the territorial integrity of the Empire in the early fifth century came from the Vandals. They passed triumphantly through France, killing the Archbishop of Reims and capturing Paris, Orleans and Tours.[1] They then crossed the Pyrenees, made their way south, and settled in large numbers in Andalusia.

Their next advance was into North Africa, where they seem to have been actively welcomed by the Roman Governor, Count Boniface. In 439, under the leadership of their King, Geiseric, they captured one of their greatest prizes, the city of Carthage.

They then suffered a setback when the same Boniface made a spirited defence of Hippo. He also distinguished himself in the defence of

Marseilles. His actions received the strong approval of Placidia, who welcomed him at her court and appointed him to supreme military command.

Boniface was one of two exceptional military leaders between whom Placidia, because of their increasing rivalry, was obliged to choose. The other was Aetius. Of the two Procopius wrote: 'There were two Roman generals, Aetius and Boniface, especially valiant men and in experience of many wars inferior to none of that time at least. These two came to be at variance in regard to matters of state, but they attained to such a degree of high-mindedness and excellence in every respect that if one should call either of them "the last of the Romans" he would not err, so true was it that all the excellent qualities of the Romans were summed up in these two men.'

Of the two Placidia preferred Boniface. Gibbon, with the spirited partisanship that was not the least of the many exhilarating features of his historical writing, concurred in this judgement. But it was Aetius who became the more powerful and successful soldier.

Their rivalry led to open conflict in Italy. This might have developed into a prolonged civil war had not Boniface received a wound, from which he later died. After that Aetius, the man against whom Attila would have to exercise his military skills, had no serious contender within the Empire.

Aetius had an unusual upbringing. In his youth he was a hostage, not only of the Huns, but also of Alaric. This experience of the ways of life of other peoples contributed significantly to his understanding of how to assess their military strengths and how to deal with them politically. It was a form of education not dissimilar to that which Placidia had during the years she spent in Gaul with the Visigoths.

An appreciative description of Aetius's appearance and qualities was given in the sixth century by the Frankish historian, St Gregory of Tours: 'He was of middle height, of manly condition, well shaped so that his body was neither too weak nor too weighty, active in limb, a most dexterous horseman, skilled in shooting the arrow, and strong in using the spear.'

In addition to these qualities which made him 'an excellent warrior', he was, Gregory wrote, 'famous in the arts of peace: free from avarice and greed, endowed with mental virtues, one who never deviated at the instance of evil instigation from his own purpose, most patient of wrongs, a lover of work, dauntless in perils, able to endure the hardships of hunger, thirst and sleeplessness.'[2]

This may seem an excessive panegyric, but it is indicative of the reputation Aetius enjoyed that two historians of very different backgrounds should have praised him so highly. Gregory was a Frankish bishop, administrator and diplomat, Procopius a Byzantine lawyer. Both were writing about a century after Aetius's death. Yet another sixth-century historian, Jordanes, went so far as to write that Aetius was born for the salvation of the Roman Empire.

Aetius's earliest military successes were achieved in France. In these, as in later campaigns, he depended largely on the support of what might today be described as minority groups. Among them were the Alans, whom he enabled to settle in large numbers in the Rhone area south of Lyons, and who consistently provided him with valuable fighting troops.[3]

One threat to the peace in Gaul came from the Franks, who, after remaining peacefully for several decades in the Meuse-Scheldt area, advanced southward and westward. Aetius's forces defeated them decisively near Arles.

Aetius made a satisfactory treaty with the powerful Vandal king Geiseric, which protected him from attack from Africa and left him free to deal with the threat posed by the Visigoths. In his dealings with them, helped perhaps by the fact that he had a Gothic wife, he showed exceptional skill.

One of his subordinate commanders, Count Litorius, who had badly underestimated the Visigoths' military capacity, was ignominiously led in triumph through the streets of Toulouse.[4] Yet not long afterwards Aetius was able to establish a close relationship with the new Visigoth king, Theodoric, who had succeeded Walia and who was to be Aetius's closest ally in the greatest battle he ever had to fight.

One of the most important of Aetius's alliances was with the Huns, whose military skills he exploited both to his own and to the Empire's advantage. It was with a Hun army that he gained the most overwhelming victory of his entire military career.

This was against the Burgundians, who had advanced from their territory in the Rhineland around Worms. Of the battle that took place contemporary accounts are extremely thin. The *Gallic Chronicle* for the year 436 recorded simply: 'A memorable war broke out against the nation of the Burgundians, in which almost all the nation, with its king, was wiped out by Aetius.' Another contemporary chronicle recorded that 'Aetius crushed in battle Gunther, the King of the Burgundians.' It added: 'The Huns utterly destroyed him with all his people.'[5]

These terse comments were to be elaborated in later centuries in some of the most famous of European legends. They were the source of much of the happenings recorded in the *Nibelungenlied* and found a new expression too in the Scandinavian *Edda*. 'Of all the Burgundian warriors,' the Nibelungen chronicler wrote, 'none was now left save that solitary pair: Gunther and Hagen.'[6]

That chroniclers were still writing about the events centuries after they took place, and doing so from information based on hearsay, suggests that the battle, and the total destruction inflicted, must have made an extraordinary impression on public awareness. As a military power the Burgundians were crippled. They were offered, and probably glad to accept, territory in Savoy and the Geneva area, where they settled.

Placidia did not altogether trust Aetius. She suspected him, probably rightly, of having at one time supported a soldier named John, whom the army in Rome had proclaimed Emperor as a rival to Placidia's young son, Valentinian. John's power, such as it was, lasted only eighteen months. His end, according to Procopius, was a gruesome one. 'Against this John Theodosius, the son of Arcadius, sent a great army and wrested from him the tyranny and gave over the royal power to Valentinian, who was still a child. Valentinian took John alive, and he brought him out in the hippodrome of Aquileia with one of his hands cut off and caused him to ride in state on an ass, and then, after he had suffered much ill treatment from the stage performers there, both in word and in deed, he put him to death.'

After John's death Aetius's own position was for a time precarious, and it was then that he turned to the Huns for support. Once he had a considerable Hun army under command his position was almost unassailable. He held the consulship no fewer than three times.

Placidia was wise and experienced enough to accept Aetius's standing, and, whatever his attitude towards the usurper John may have been, he seems, during the decade and more when so much was done to restore the stability of the Western Empire, to have remained consistently loyal to Placidia and to Valentinian.

Placidia continued to exercise much of the power after Valentinian was old enough to succeed. She was accused by Procopius of deliberately bringing her son up to be effeminate, dissolute and superstitious. Apart from the inherent improbability of such a statement, which has no supporting evidence, Valentinian was not without redeeming qualities. He was weak, but this was not surprising. Only the females among Theodosius I's children and grandchildren inherited his strength of character.

Placidia died in 450, her death coinciding roughly with the moment when Attila made his decision to invade the Western Empire. She was in Rome when her death occurred, and her body does not seem to have been brought to the mausoleum that was built in Ravenna during her lifetime and under her instructions.

As a monument it is exquisite. In the cupola concentric gold stars are set against a dark blue background, with the figure of the cross dominating the whole. The walls are partly faced with yellow marble, on to which light is filtered through windows made of paper-thin alabaster. The figures in the mosaics include St Peter and St Paul, both wearing white togas in the manner of Roman senators, and two doves, one drinking and one approaching a fountain.

The symbolism is wholly religious in intent, yet some of the figures depicted in mosaic may also suggest the character of a woman inspired by faith, yet with a clear understanding of how empires are governed and how peace can be successfully maintained.

CHAPTER 15

PROPOSAL OF MARRIAGE

Whether Attila seriously considered a full-scale invasion of Persia, as was thought likely in the well-informed circles in which Priscus moved, is not known. A considerable force of Hun cavalry was sent to help the Armenians, who were rebelling against Persian rule, but they were unable to prevent a major defeat which the Armenians suffered in 451.[1] After that Attila made no serious effort to involve himself in Persian affairs.

Nor do we know when he first examined the alternative strategy of invading the Western Empire. No doubt he discussed this with the various Westerners in his entourage, and he probably took soundings of the ambassadors from the West who visited him.

One fact which is known is that a sudden impetus was given to his intentions by an extraordinary proposal he received from Galla Placidia's daughter, Honoria.

Honoria was yet another of Theodosius I's female descendants of spirit and independence of mind. She had the title of Augusta conferred on her when she was little more than a girl and when her status was no more than that of Emperor's sister.[2] It seems likely that Placidia saw in her a future successor to her own position provided a suitable husband could be found.

She had her own establishment within the palace precincts in Ravenna and a chamberlain to manage it. In the inimitable words of Gibbon, 'in the midst of vain and unsatisfactory pomp Honoria sighed, yielded to the impulse of her nature, and threw herself into the arms of her chamberlain Eugenius. Her guilt and shame (such is the absurd language of imperious man) were soon betrayed by the appearance of pregnancy.'

Being an ambitious young woman, she decided the best way out of her predicament would be to have Eugenius made Emperor. Once Valentinian realized what her intentions were he responded by having Eugenius put to death. He was then faced with the problem of what to do with Honoria.

An attempt was made to force her into a betrothal to a rich senator named Flavius Bassus Herculanus, who, it was felt, could be relied on not to have any imperial ambitions. This suggestion had no appeal for Honoria, and Placidia decided that there was only one place where she could be kept in safety and without disturbing the peace in Ravenna. This was Constantinople, to which she herself had retreated when her position in Ravenna had seemed insecure. Once there Honoria found herself under the relentless supervision of Pulcheria and her virgin sisters.

After what must have seemed an eternity of prayer and fasting, Honoria entrusted a Constantinople eunuch named Hyacinth with a secret mission. He was to take her gold ring and present it to Attila. This constituted a proposal of marriage, as Attila fully understood.

No doubt Honoria was prepared to go to considerable lengths to escape from the regime of Pulcheria. She had too the knowledge of her mother's acceptable marriage to someone considered a barbarian king. But it is reasonable to suppose that her primary concerns were dynastic and political. A union between the Empress's sister and the ruler of an important kingdom could, she no doubt felt, be exploited to great advantage.

Attila saw the proposal in a similar light. He was already plentifully supplied with wives, but Honoria's advances fitted his own plans in a way he could hardly have hoped for. He accepted her proposal of marriage, adding, with splendid panache, that the dowry he expected to go with it was half the Western Roman Empire.

When Theodosius learnt what Honoria had done he was appalled. He had consistently pursued a policy of trying to appease the Huns by buying them off, and he dreaded the prospect of Attila marching on Constantinople once again, this time demanding Honoria as his bride. He therefore sent Honoria back to Ravenna together with Hyacinth.

He also wrote to Valentinian advising him to hand Honoria over and accede to Attila's demands. It was the last major gesture of appeasement he was to make before meeting with his fatal riding accident.

Valentinian's reaction was very different. He had Hyacinth subjected to torture, when all the details of his mission were revealed, and then had him executed. He was even more enraged with his sister, and only Placidia's intercession seems to have saved Honoria's life.[3]

After that Valentinian had to rely on his own judgement. Galla Placidia, on whom he had long been dependent, and Theodosius, an experienced statesman, both died in 450, and it was in that year that Attila's demands had to be met or rejected. Valentinian decided on rejection, and Attila in turn decided on war.

Valentinian's reactions were in some respects similar to those of his uncle, Honorius, when confronted by Alaric's demands. Both were weak men showing defiance. But there were differences in the circumstances. Honorius, for much of the time, had no effective means of resisting Alaric. Valentinian had an accomplished general in Aetius, who commanded considerable forces. In the circumstances his refusal to treat with Attila was not unreasonable. What he almost certainly did not know was the strength of the army that Attila would be able to muster.

This army was in fact a racially mixed one and included Gepids, Ostrogoths, Skirians, Swabians and Alemans. Because of the absence of the Hun forces in Armenia it was almost certainly more Germanic than Hun in composition.[4] It was also comparatively slow-moving.

The Romans had built a road from what are today the outskirts of Budapest to Vienna, and it is reasonable to assume that Attila's army followed it.[5] There are no contemporary literary accounts showing the exact route taken by the army before it reached France. Legends do however provide some guidance.

The *Nibelungenlied* tells of continual passage between Worms and Hungary along the Rhine and Danube. Rüdiger, who in the *Nibelungenlied* is the chief emissary from the Burgundians to the Huns, was said to have come from Pochlarn in the Wachau. Such evidence and the facts of geography suggest that the army advanced along the Danube through the area now dominated by vineyards and castles.

Then there was the colourful legend of St Ursula, who, rather than marry the man chosen for her by her royal father, opted for perpetual virginity. In pursuit of this ideal she set off on a journey by sea together with eleven thousand other virgins. The source of this supply has not been clearly established, but it is thought to have been Britain.

The ship in which they sailed ran aground on the Dutch coast, but was able to continue the journey up the Rhine to Cologne. There Ursula was visited by an angel, who instructed her to continue up-river with her companions to Basle, and from there to cross the Alps on foot and make their pilgrimage to Rome. The angel also informed her that on their return to Cologne they would suffer martyrdom.

On reaching Cologne again after their pilgrimage Ursula and her companions found it occupied by a Hun army. The King of the Huns proposed marriage to Ursula, and when she refused he killed her with an arrow. Her eleven thousand companions also suffered the martyrdom that had been promised.[6]

There is no archaeological evidence that Attila's army ever came to Cologne.[7] Nor have any artefacts of unmistakably Hun origin been found near the Danube in Austria.[8] But this negative evidence is of little consequence, as advancing armies would not have left behind them the kind of artefacts that have come to light in the graves of Hun princes and nobles. The legends do at least suggest that memories of the passage of Attila's army were preserved for a long time.

Attila's primary reason for advancing into the Rhineland seems to have been in order to join forces with the Franks, with whom he was in alliance. At some point, which has not been established, his army crossed the Rhine. It then followed the line of the Moselle.

It is probable, though not altogether certain, that Attila's army took possession of the important city of Trier on the Moselle, the residence of emperors, which had been fortified by Augustus and was known as Roma Secunda. The Franks had earlier sacked the city and they were to establish themselves firmly there four years after Attila's invasion. One early report mentions Attila's occupation of the city,[9] and it seems likely that this was a direct consequence of his alliance with the Franks.

Further up the Moselle lay Metz, another important military and ecclesiastical centre, which Julius Caesar had described as one of the oldest and most important towns in Gaul. There was no easy way of capturing Metz, and the siege of the city began on 7 April 451.

In the words of Gregory of Tours, 'the Huns, issuing from Pannonia, reached the town of Metz on the vigil of the feast of Easter, devastating the whole country. They gave the city to the flames and slew the people with the edge of the sword, and did to death the priests of the Lord before the holy altars.'

One building, according to Gregory, was spared. This was the oratory of the deacon, Stephen. Of it Gregory wrote: 'The blessed deacon Stephen, conferring with the holy apostles Peter and Paul about this destruction, said: "I beseech you suffer not the city of Metz to be burned to the ground by the enemy."'

The deacon conceded that the evil deeds of the people might be such that the city would have to be destroyed, but he asked that his oratory at least might be spared. To this the apostles replied: 'Go in peace, most beloved brother, this oratory of thine alone shall be spared in the fire. For the city we shall not obtain this grace, seeing that the sentence of divine judgement is already gone forth upon it. The sin of the people is grown so great, and the sound of their wickedness is gone up before the Lord. For this cause shall this city be burned with fire.'

The happenings in Metz around Easter 451, both the destruction and the avoidance of destruction, were a foretaste of much that was to occur as Attila's army advanced through France. City after city, we learn from the Christian chroniclers, suffered destruction as a punishment for the sins of the people. Where destruction and death are avoided it is due to divine response to the supplications and conduct of the pious.

Nowhere is it suggested that Attila's armies conquered through superior military skills. His own part is that of an instrument of punishment, the Scourge of God.

CHAPTER 16

INVASION OF FRANCE

The areas of Germany and France through which Attila's army passed had already lost much of the cohesion that they had long enjoyed following Julius Caesar's conquest of Gaul.

Over some four centuries Roman civilization had penetrated deeply and widely through Transalpine Gaul, the territory comprising modern France and Belgium together with parts of Germany, the Netherlands and Switzerland.

In parts of southern France, the area known as Gallia Narbonensis, the Romans superimposed their own culture on cities that had long before been colonized and civilized by Greeks. Elsewhere, in the provinces of Aquitaine, Lugdunensis (the land lying roughly between the Loire and the Seine) and Belgica, the process of Romanization was slower, the Celtic language, for instance, persisting for some centuries. But the Romans did not find it necessary to garrison these territories.

The peace was disturbed from time to time, particularly in the third century, but until the early fifth century Gaul was successfully protected from foreign invasion by Roman armies entrenched behind fortified lines which ran from Cologne to Regensburg.

The Vandals and the Visigoths, the Franks and the Burgundians changed all this. Military and political control became fluid. Allegiances were transferred from one centre of power and protection to another. Where fighting took place the masses of the peasantry may have had difficulty in distinguishing between the contestants.

There were certain focal points of resistance to Attila's army as it advanced. Most of them were in the larger, fortified towns, and in these the bishop was likely to play a leading role. But it would be misleading to regard the progress of Attila's army primarily as the invasion of one sovereign state by the forces of another, comparable, for example, with those of Belgium and, later, of Poland by German armies in the twentieth century.

The forces on both sides were too heterogeneous for such a comparison to be more than superficial. In consequence the war, as it developed, became more and more a contest between the two leaders, Attila and Aetius, for it was they who had to retain the support and loyalty of the fighting men by strategic skill, diplomatic finesse, personality and, not least, by providing them with the loot that they expected.

Many fine cities confronted Attila's army as it advanced, Trier and Metz among them. French scholars have been at pains in recent years to try to establish the exact route the army followed after it left Metz and before it reached Orléans.

The Visigoths nearly half a century earlier were known to have advanced through Arras, Amiens, Reims and Paris before reaching Orléans and Tours. The line of Attila's advance was certainly different, and in one recent study it was suggested that, rather than taking Roman roads, the army may have followed a much more ancient route along river beds, where better pasturage would have been available. This would have taken it south of Verdun, Reims and Paris.[1]

Other commentators, Gregory of Tours among them, have stated that Attila's army sacked Reims, which for some centuries had been an important city and was already a centre of the champagne industry. This may not, however, have been the case.

People known as the Remi had early come to terms with the Romans, and a bishopric had been established in their city in the third century. Later, in the fifth century, when Clovis, King of the Franks, was baptized in Reims by St Remigius, the oil required for the ceremony was reputed to have been brought by a dove from Heaven. That such an important Christian city should have attracted the attention of Attila's army would have been a natural assumption for later chroniclers to make. In reality there may have been some confusion in their accounts between Attila's invasion and the earlier one by Visigoths.

Mundane considerations such as pasturage may well have decided Attila's route, but ecclesiastical chroniclers tended to attribute it rather to divine intervention. Gregory of Tours cited a number of examples of people who, through prayer or piety, were spared direct encounter with the Huns. One was Bishop Servais of Tongres, who was more generally credited with having died towards the end of the fourth century.

When reports spread that the Huns were about to invade Gaul, Servais, who, according to Gregory, passed his time in praying and fasting, 'begged God in His mercy not to allow this incredible people, who were altogether unworthy of the Lord, to enter Gaul.' He was told that, because of the sins of the people, it had been decided that the Huns would not only enter Gaul but would 'devastate it in the manner of a great hurricane.'

For his part he was advised to put his house in order, prepare his burial place and find a winding sheet. 'In this way you will leave your earthly body, and your eyes will not witness the evils which the Huns will perpetrate in Gaul.'

A less important city than Trier, Metz or Reims, which also had some reason to fear an attack by Attila's army, was Paris. Known to the Romans as Lutetia, Paris was for some centuries little more than a fortified island on the Seine, the present site of the Île de la Cité.

For the Emperor Julian, at least, it had considerable charm. 'I happened to be in winter quarters', he wrote, 'at my beloved Lutetia – for that is how the Celts call the capital of the Parisians. It is a small island lying in the river. A wall entirely surrounds it, and wooden bridges lead to it on both sides. The river seldom rises and falls, but usually is the same depth in the winter as in the summer season, and it provides water which is very clear to the eye and very pleasant for one who wishes to drink. As the inhabitants live on an island they have to draw their water chiefly from the river.'

He was probably fortunate in the weather he experienced, for one reason why Paris was of little importance as a fortress was that it was subject to periodic flooding.

'The winter', Julian wrote, 'is rather mild there, perhaps from the warmth of the ocean, which is not more than nine hundred states distant, and it may be that a slight breeze from the water is wafted so far, for sea water seems to be warmer than fresh. Whether from this or from some other cause obscure to me, the fact is, as I say, that those who live in that place have a warmer winter. A good kind of vine grows thereabouts, and some people have even managed to make fig trees grow by covering them in winter with a sort of garment of wheat straw and with things of that sort such as are used to protect trees from the harm that is done to them by the cold air.'[2]

Among the inhabitants of Paris was a girl named Geneviève, who came from Auxerre, where, at the age of seven, she had been persuaded by its Bishop, St Germain, to dedicate herself to a life of faith. After her parents' death she came to Paris, where too she distinguished herself by austerity and works of benevolence.

When rumours began to circulate that Attila's army was approaching Paris, Geneviève was reported to have rallied the population in a way no one else was capable of doing. In one of the churches she offered, in front of the whole congregation, to go alone or at the head of a group of virgins such as herself to confront the barbarian leader. She also prophesied that Paris would be spared from any attack by Attila, a prophecy that proved correct.

Geneviève became the patron saint of Paris, and her spirit was to be invoked at different times in the future when Paris was threatened. One such occasion occurred in 1915, when the director of the *Revue Hebdomadaire* likened Attila to King William II of Prussia and called them both the Scourge of God.

'Attila, King of the Huns,' the director wrote, 'claimed to be the emissary of a superior power of terror and barbarism which had sent him to chastise those who opposed his wishes. Attila said that grass no longer grew under the feet of his horse, and the Prussian said that he would have his horse drinking the water of the Seine on 15th August.

'Attila did reach the walls of Paris, spreading fire, like William, along his way. But a girl, she who became the patroness of Paris, Geneviève, gave courage to its inhabitants. From the top of a hill near here, where her cult and her memory are preserved, she encouraged the Parisians and called upon them not to abandon Paris. In the face of this masculine [sic] assurance Attila turned away from the city.'[3]

St Geneviève had a counterpart in Troyes in the person of its Bishop, St Loup, who held office for more than fifty years from 426 to 479.

Gregory of Tours wrote of him: 'In 451 the savage Attila, King of his Huns, who had already destroyed Reims, Langres, Besançon and several other cities, marched on Troyes. The whole town was in a state of fear. The Bishop, St Loup, decided to save his people. After praying and fasting he donned his pontifical garb and, full of confidence in God, left the town to meet the barbarians.

'When he came to the King of the Huns he asked: "Who are you?" Attila replied: "I am the Scourge of God." "If indeed you are the Scourge of God," the saint said, "do only that which God allows you." Struck by these words and the saintliness of the Bishop, the barbarian kept his promise to the disappointment of his hordes, who were avid for blood and plunder.'

This encounter between St Loup and Attila gave rise to a work of art of striking beauty. In 1503 Nicholas Forget, Abbot of the church in Troyes dedicated to St Loup, commissioned a local goldsmith, Jean Papillon, and a Limoges artist, Nardon Pénicaud, to produce a series of enamels, which can be seen today in Troyes Cathedral.

The first shows a meeting between Attila and St Loup's deacon, Memon, accompanied by seven young priests. All are reputed to have been massacred by the Huns. In the second St Loup buries the murdered men. In the third he parleys with Attila at the city gates. Whether the murder of the priests was a historical fact or a local accretion to the Attila legend is open to question.[4]

After referring briefly to such reports of divine intervention Gibbon caustically observed: 'As the greatest part of the Gallic cities were alike destitute of saints and soldiers they were besieged and stormed by the Huns, who practised their customary maxims of war.' Yet the only city that he, like other historians, specified as having suffered almost total destruction was Metz. From this, and from the examples of cities that were spared, it may well be assumed that the campaign was no more damaging than those of other invading forces. The army no doubt lived from the land and plundered where it readily could, but wanton destruction may not have been extensive.

There is no clear evidence to show how far Attila intended to go in the course of his campaign in France, but it is more than probable that his principal objective was Toulouse. Although a relatively unimportant place in the early years of Roman rule in Gaul, Toulouse had been made the capital of the Visigoth kingdom in 419, and it was there that King Theodoric, who, together with Aetius, was to lead the main forces opposing Attila's army, held his court.

After advancing south for some time, Attila's army encountered strong, and perhaps unexpected, resistance at Orléans. In an earlier campaign Aetius had garrisoned Orléans with a considerable force of mercenaries, including Huns and Alans, and the city remained a fortress. Here too there was a religious leader of power and personality, a fit subject for the admiration of Gregory of Tours.

'Attila, King of the Huns,' this enthusiastic chronicler wrote, 'came to Orléans and battered it with rams, striving so to take the city. At that time the most blessed Anianus was Bishop in the city, a man eminent in wisdom and renowned for holiness, the record of whose virtuous deeds are faithfully preserved among us. When the beleaguered people cried out to their Bishop what they should do, he, trusting in God, enjoined them to prostrate themselves in prayer.'

This they did, and while they were praying the Bishop said: 'Look forth from the city wall, if haply the pity of God succour us.'

Anianus had visited Aetius in Arles and knew something of his intentions. In consequence he expected a relieving army to reach Orléans before long. The people looked from the city wall, as instructed, but saw nothing to comfort them. Gregory continued: 'Again with many tears and lamentations they besought the compassion of the Lord. But when their prayer was done, they looked forth from the wall a third time, as the old man bade them, and behold they saw afar off, as it might be a cloud rising from the earth. And they brought the Bishop the news, and he said: "It is the succour of the Lord." The walls were already shaking under the shock of the rams, and on the point of falling, when behold Aetius came, and Theodoric, King of the Goths, and Thorismond, his son, with their armies.'

The decisive action in Attila's campaign in France was about to begin.

CHAPTER 17

BATTLE IS JOINED

The successful resistance of the city of Orléans was a new and disturbing experience for Attila. In his campaigns in the Balkans and through Germany and France he had become accustomed to cities that surrendered to him or which could be destroyed at his will. Only Constantinople, with its virtually impregnable walls, had been unattainable.

For the conquest of Orléans, moreover, he had expected the support of a powerful fifth column. This was to have come from Sangiban, King of the Alans, who had secretly promised to deliver both Arles, which he occupied for some time, and Orléans to Attila. His plan was revealed to Aetius and foiled.

For some time before Attila's army reached Orléans it had been clear to the Romans that the only force that could effectively resist him was one that Aetius had brought over the Alps. Even this, to have any chance of success, would have to be heavily reinforced by alliances formed in Gaul. Whether these would be forthcoming remained doubtful almost up to the moment of engagement in battle. The crucial problem was the stance to be taken by the Visigoths.

The Visigoth king, Theodoric I, who was the son of Alaric, had by then reigned for more than thirty years and had established a firm rule over a people who, adapting themselves to Roman ways, were developing an interesting indigenous culture. A vivid description of the Visigoth court was given by Bishop Sidonius, the founder of a new city at Mainz, who was closely acquainted with Theodoric's son, Theodoric II.

Of Theodoric II's appearance Sidonius wrote: 'The upper ears are buried under underlying locks, after the fashion of his race. The nose is finely aquiline. His barber is assiduous in eradicating the rich growth on the lower part of the face.'

Sidonius went on: 'Before daybreak he goes with a very small suite to attend the service of his priests. He prays with assiduity, but, if I may speak in confidence, one may suspect more from habit than conviction in his piety. Administrative duties of the kingdom take up the rest of the morning. Armed nobles stand about the royal seat. The mass of guards in their garb of skins are admitted so that they may be within call, but kept at the threshold for quiet's sake. Now the foreign envoys are introduced. The King hears them out, but says little. If a thing needs more discussion he puts it off, but accelerates matters ripe for despatch.' By the time all this was completed it was seven o'clock in the morning, and King Theodoric then inspected his treasure chamber or stables.

'On ordinary days', the Bishop wrote, 'his table resembles that of a private person. The board does not groan beneath a mass of dull and unpolished silver set on by panting servitors. The weight lies rather in the conversation than in the plate. There is either sensible talk or none. The hangings and draperies used on these occasions are sometimes of purple silk, sometimes only of linen. Art, not costliness, commands the fare, as spotlessness rather than bulk the silver. Toasts are few, and you will oftener see a thirsty guest impatient than a full one refusing cup or bowl.'

After a short siesta, and perhaps a break for dice, work would resume at three in the afternoon. 'Back come the importunates, back the ushers to remove them. On all sides buzz the voices of petitioners, a sound which lasts till evening and does not diminish till interrupted by the royal repast. Even then they only disperse to attend their various patrons among the courtiers and are astir till bedtime.'[1]

For such a kingdom, waging war might be deemed a necessity, but it was no longer a way of life, and, as reports were received of the advance of Attila's army, Theodoric I, a shrewd as well as experienced ruler, had to decide whether he had more to gain by an alliance with Aetius or by one with Attila. He and Aetius had earlier been in dispute over the possession of Arles, when Aetius had been successful, and as he marched his army through Lyons Aetius learned that the

Visigoths intended to join forces with Attila if and when he reached their territory.

Fortunately for Aetius there was a retired senator living in Auvergne named Avitus, who, he believed, could serve as the perfect intermediary between Imperial Rome and the Visigoth Kingdom. Avitus accepted the task given him and made his way to Toulouse.

There he spoke with great eloquence, describing the devastation that the Huns had caused in the past and would no doubt inflict on the Visigoth Kingdom. He dwelt on the need to protect fields and vineyards and appealed to the Visigoths as Christians, albeit of the Arian persuasion, to save churches and relics from sacrilege and violation. In this way his mission succeeded. In the words of Gibbon: 'Theodoric yielded to the evidence of truth, adopted the measure at once the most prudent and the most honourable, and declared that as the faithful ally of Aetius and the Romans he was ready to expose his life and kingdom for the common safety of Gaul.'

Theodoric's decision influenced a number of soldiers of various races who had settled in Gaul to join Aetius's army, and eventually Aetius had under his command Alans, Burgundians, Franks, Saxons and others. But the Visigoths were his most important recruits. They came as an allied rather than a subordinate force. In the event this distinction was to be significant.

Once the siege of Orléans had been raised it was clear to Attila that he would have to engage in a major battle, and, in accordance with normal custom, he called upon his shamanite priests to foretell the outcome. They duly examined the entrails of cattle and streaks to be seen in scraped bones, and came to an alarming conclusion. The Huns, they declared, would meet with disaster.

They did, however, make another prophecy. This was that the commander of the opposing force would be killed in battle, a happening that would mar the ultimate victory. Attila, understandably, assumed that the priests were foretelling the death of Aetius.

The choice of battlefield was made by Attila. With the large cosmopolitan army, which he now commanded, he knew he had to engage in a very different kind of warfare from that which his ancestors had known. He could not rely on the unexpected lightning attack, feigned retreat and renewed attack by small groups of expert horsemen-archers. He now had to pay as much attention to defence as to attack. Nevertheless he wanted an open terrain on which his cavalry could operate to advantage, and in search of this he advanced slowly northwards and crossed the Seine.

Aetius's army followed, and as it did so a preliminary battle broke out between his vanguard, consisting of Franks, and Attila's rearguard, which was made up largely of Gepids. It was a short but fierce encounter. Jordanes, no doubt exaggerating, claimed that fifteen thousand men were killed.

The exact site of the main battlefield has still not been determined with certainty, archaeologists and historians continuing to advance differing opinions. In early accounts the names 'Mauriacus' and 'Campus Cathaulaunicus' were both used. 'Cathaulaunicus' meant 'belonging to the city of Châlons', and for this reason the engagement has come to be known variously as the Battle of Châlons and the Battle of the Catalaunian Fields. One expert considers it to have taken place near the village of Maucourt,[2] another at a site some seven to eight kilometres west of Troyes.[3]

An earlier historian of the battle, Sir Edward Creasy, wrote of the battle taking place among long rows of poplars, through which the river Marne wound its way, and a few scattered villages, which alone varied the monotony of the landscape.

Before the main battle was joined there was an unfortunate episode when a priest from the camp of the Ostrogoths, who were fighting on Attila's side, visited the Visigoths, accompanied by some followers. Because of the sunlight glinting on them the crosses they carried were mistaken for shields, and the Visigoths let fire with their arrows. The priest, whose name was Mesmin, was killed, and he was declared a martyr. A memorial was later erected by an unlearned local community, on which appeared the curious name 'St Memorius'.

Another preliminary to action was the speech made by Attila to his troops. According to Jordanes, his words were: 'Here you stand after conquering mighty nations and subduing the world. I therefore think it foolish for me to goad you with words, as though you were men who had not been proved in action. Let a new leader or an untried army resort to that. It is not right for me to say anything common, nor ought you to listen. For what is war but your usual custom? Or what is sweeter for a brave man than to seek revenge with his own hand? It is a right of nature to glut the soul with vengeance. Let us then attack the foe eagerly, for they are ever the bolder who make the attack.'

Surprisingly perhaps, in view of the composition of his own army, Attila, according to Jordanes, continued: 'Despise this union of discordant races. To defend oneself by alliance is proof of cowardice. See, even before our attack, they are smitten with terror. They seek the heights, they seize the hills and, repenting too late, clamour for protection against battle in the open fields.'

Contrasting traditional Roman and Hun methods of warfare, Attila was said to have continued: 'You know how slight a matter the Roman attack is. While they are still gathering in order and forming in one line with locked shields, they are checked, I will not say by the first wound, but even by the dust of battle. Then on to the fray with stout hearts, as is your wont. Despise their battle line. Attack the Alans, smite the Visigoths. Seek swift victory in that spot where the battle rages, for when the sinews are cut the limbs soon relax, nor can a body stand when you have taken away the bones. Let your courage rise and your own fury burst forth.'

The remainder of the speech was purely that of a Hun leader addressing Hun compatriots. 'Now show your cunning, Huns, now your deeds of arms. Let the wounded exact in return the death of his foe. Let the unwounded revel in slaughter of the enemy. No spear shall harm those who are sure to live, and those who are sure to die fate overtakes even in peace. And, finally, why should fortune have made the Huns victorious over so many nations unless it were to prepare them for the joy of this conflict?

'Who was it revealed to our sires the path through the Maeotian swamp, for so many ages a closed secret? Who made armed men yield to you when you were as yet unarmed? Even a mass of federated nations could not endure the sight of the Huns. I am not deceived in this issue. Here is the field so many victories have promised us.'

Attila's final words, according to Jordanes, were not those of a Hun archer and rider, but rather those of a conventional Roman warrior. 'I shall hurl the first spear at the foe. If any man can stand at rest while Attila fights, he is a dead man.'

CHAPTER 18

THE CATALAUNIAN FIELDS

The battle of the Catalaunian Fields was fought towards the end of June 451. It has been described as one of the fifteen decisive battles of the world.[1]

It was an international conflict, in which exceptionally large forces were engaged. Gibbon wrote that 'the nations from the Volga to the Atlantic were assembled on the plain of Chalons.' The sixth-century Ostrogoth scholar and administrator Cassiodorus described the battle as 'a conflict fierce, various, obstinate and bloody, such as could not be paralleled either in the present or in past ages.'[2]

It was also a contest between the two greatest military leaders of their time, men who had much in common and who had abundant reasons to respect each other. Their upbringings had been similar, Aetius as a privileged hostage among Huns, Attila as a Hun prince. Aetius, no less than Attila, understood how to use Hun troops to advantage. Both men not only knew how to command the loyalty of a cosmopolitan army, but were obliged to do so for their very survival. Both had shown themselves to be skilled diplomats as well as military strategists. When they met in battle each probably found it easy to read the other's mind.

The battle took place on predominantly level ground, but there was a small hill, initially occupied by Aetius's forces, which was to be hotly disputed. Attila's Huns occupied a central position. To their right were the Gepids, commanded by Attila's faithful ally, King Ardaric. On the left were the Ostrogoths, led by three brothers, on the eldest of whom, Walamir, Attila also placed considerable reliance. Jordanes described him as a good keeper of secrets, bland of speech and skilled in wiles.

The other elements in Attila's army were held in reserve or scattered

Medallion showing the head of Attila, from the Charterhouse in Parma, Italy

Engraving of the French actor Geoffroy (1804–1895) in the role of Attila

Attila from an engraving published in London, 1810

Attila, advancing against Paris, from the painting by Delaunay

Attila at the Battle of Chalons

Another view of the Battle of Châlons. From a French publication,
Cents Recits de l'Histoire de France (1878)

The Huns of Attila, by the 19th century Spanish artist Checa

A still from the French film *La Horde des Huns*, directed by Fritz Lang, 1924

Attila meets Pope Leo. A wall painting from the Vatican by Raphael

The saddle of a Hun horseman, reconstructed on the basis of archaeological evidence

Rudolf Klein-Rogga in the role of Attila, from the film *La Vengeance de Kriemhilde* (1924)

Anthony Quinn in the title role of *Attila, Scourge of God* (1954)

Kurt Rydle in the title role of Verdi's *Attila* (Theatre du Chatelet, Paris 1982)

among the principal fighting formations. As Jordanes put it, 'the rest of the crowd of kings, if we may call them so, and the leaders of various nations hung upon Attila's nod like slaves, and when he gave a sign, even by a glance, without a murmur each stood forth in fear and trembling, or at all events did as he was bid. Attila alone was king of all kings over all and concerned for all.'

On the opposing side Aetius commanded the right wing and Theodoric, with his Visigoths, the left. In the centre, where he could be kept under observation, was King Sangiban, who commanded the Alans, but whose loyalty Aetius had reason to doubt.

Attila's army began by discharging a large number of arrows, and a cavalry engagement followed. The Huns and their allies gained an initial advantage by breaking through in the centre. Then they wheeled and attacked the Visigoths.

The hand-to-hand fighting was, in Jordanes's words, 'fierce, confused, monstrous, unrelenting.' He even wrote that a stream was turned into a torrent by the flow of human blood and that 'those whose wounds drove them to slake their parching thirst drank water mingled with gore.'

King Theodoric rode among his men, encouraging them to hold on, but he was thrown from his horse. One report stated that he was trampled by the horses of his own army, another that he was struck by an Ostrogoth's spear. All that was known for certain was that he died on the battlefield. When the news of this reached him later Attila understood that his soothsayer's prophecy of the death of the opposing leader related not to Aetius, but to Theodoric.

Attila's first objective remained the small hill, which the enemy forces occupied. The engagement between Huns and Alans in the centre was indecisive, and the main encounter on the first day was between Visigoths and Ostrogoths. Theodoric's son Thorismund took over the command of the Visigoths; the Ostrogoths were driven back; and Attila, in danger of being outflanked, was forced to retreat. The hill, fought for with so much loss of life, had not been taken.

Defences had been prepared in the form of trenches and wagons, and Attila's army had to take up new positions behind them. The archers were able to repulse further attacks from Visigoth cavalry, and the defensive position was held. But in every respect Attila's offensive had failed, and he had no immediate chance of renewing it. Victory, although not decisive, had gone to the armies of Aetius and the Visigoths.

Theodoric's body was eventually discovered. 'After a long search,' Jordanes wrote, 'they found him where the dead lay thickest, as happens with brave men. They honoured him with songs and bore him away in the sight of the enemy. You might have seen bands of Goths shouting with dissonant cries and paying the honours of death while the battle still raged. Tears were shed, but such as they were accustomed to devote to brave men.'

Attila decided that he must prepare for the worst eventuality. This was not death, but capture, and he therefore had his own funeral pyre prepared. Wooden saddles and other cavalry accoutrements were piled up, ready to be set ablaze if necessary. Attila, Jordanes wrote, 'remained supremely brave even in this extremity. He was determined to cast himself into the flames, that none might have the joy of wounding him and that the lord of so many races might not fall into the hands of his foes.' Another report that his wives, who had accompanied him on his campaign, were to suffer the same fate lacks Jordanes's authority and may or may not have been speculation.[3]

Aetius held a council of war with Thorismund and other leaders. The decision reached was to subject Attila's forces to a prolonged siege. He was thought to have few reserves of provisions for men and animals, and archers would be placed so that they could prevent foraging parties from breaking out in search of supplies.

This may well have been a wise strategy, for the daily requirements of an army the size of Attila's were huge. Whether it would have succeeded, or whether Attila could have mounted a successful counter-attack, we shall never know because of the extraordinary decision that was in fact taken. Shortly after the siege was instituted Aetius abandoned it and withdrew his forces.

Why he did so is a question on which many have speculated, although few of the explanations given have been convincing. Jordanes's opinion, which has been endorsed by most subsequent commentators, was that Aetius, as a skilful politician, had one overriding interest. This was to maintain the balance of power after the battle which would be least damaging to the Roman Empire.

Thorismund, Jordanes wrote, 'consulted with the patrician Aetius – for he was an older man and of more mature wisdom – with regard to what he ought to do next. Aetius feared that if the Huns were totally destroyed by the Goths the Roman Empire would be overwhelmed, and urgently advised him to return to his own dominions to take up the rule which his father had left.'

As inducements Aetius advanced further arguments. If Thorismund remained on the field of battle, his brothers might seize their father's possessions and gain control over the Visigoths. In that event Thorismund would have to fight against his own countrymen with no certainty of the outcome of the struggle.

It is not impossible that this is what happened. Aetius had a long history of handling the Huns with diplomatic skill, of allying himself with them when necessary, and of using them for his own military ends. Against this it must be remembered that Jordanes was a Goth, with a strong inclination to present Goths generally – and Goth leaders in particular – in a favourable light. (The fact that, with this prejudice, he wrote so admiringly of Attila is an indication of the reputation Attila still enjoyed a century after his death.)

There is, however, another and, surely, a much likelier explanation of what occurred. Theodoric, perhaps because of Avitus's arguments, perhaps for other reasons, had decided, after some hesitation, to join forces with Aetius. There is no reason to believe that Thorismund was of the same opinion, and if a report reached him that he would be wise to return to Toulouse to look after his own interests, he could well have regretted being involved in the battle in the first instance.

The undisputed fact is that he did leave and, according to Jordanes, 'advanced in royal state and entered Tolosa. Here, although the throng of his brothers and brave companions were still rejoicing over the victory, he yet began to rule so mildly that no one strove with him for the succession to the kingdom.'

In short, the Visigoths, under Thorismund's command, abandoned their allies on the battlefield, a course of action which Jordanes, the Goth, had somehow to explain. The alternative explanation, that Thorismund's throne was coveted by one of his brothers – the one indeed whose lifestyle Sidonius described – was not only more probable than the one Jordanes advanced, it was also to be borne out by what took place later in Toulouse.

Aetius had very little cause to fear the Visigoths, who had settled peacefully in the territories they had fairly recently acquired. Nor did he have any reason to suppose that allowing Attila to retain a large army would help to preserve peace in the Roman Empire. What he did know was that without Visigoth support he would be in serious danger of defeat, just as he had been shortly after he had crossed the Alps and was still alarmingly short of allies.

In these circumstances, calling off the battle would have been a simple act of prudence. But if this interpretation is accepted, it does invite the question: who won the battle of the Catalaunian Fields?

Through the centuries historians have debated both the scale and the significance of the battle. The scale is not easy to assess. Jordanes wrote: 'In this most famous war of the bravest tribes 165,000 are said to have been slain on both sides, leaving out of account 15,000 of the Gepidae and Franks who met each other the night before the general engagement.' Other chroniclers gave the strength of Attila's army as 700,000.[4] These figures are no doubt exaggerations. Modern estimates put the total number engaged in the battle somewhere between 30,000 and 50,000.[5]

Certainly it was a major battle, and the legend that the ghosts of those who were killed continued the fight for several days indicates how it was assessed by those who endured it, and by those to whom they related their experiences.

The historian who included the battle of the Catalaunian Fields or, as he called it, the battle of Châlons among the fifteen decisive battles of the world was Sir Edward Creasy, who was appointed Professor of Modern and Ancient History in the University of London in 1840.

Creasy began his list of fifteen battles with Marathon and Syracuse. He ended it with Valmy and Waterloo. Lord D'Abernon, who was present when the Poles defeated the invading Soviet army in the outskirts of Warsaw in 1920, later added this and the battles of Sedan and the Marne to Creasy's list.[6]

The great significance of the battle of the Catalaunian Fields, in Creasy's judgement, was the extent to which it helped to shape the

Europe that succeeded the Roman Empire. Had its outcome been different, he believed, the Empire that Charlemagne founded, a Germanic and Christian one, would not have taken the shape it did.

One does not have to accept Creasy's simplifications, nor his manifest prejudices, to agree that the western Europe that Visigoths, Ostrogoths, Franks and others developed was very different from what it might have been had it passed under Hun dominion. For that matter, it would have been very different had it become part of the Byzantine Empire, as in the sixth century the Emperor Justinian sought to make it. The issue that is not clear is the extent to which the battle of the Catalaunian Fields did decide the future structure of western Europe.

For a battle that Creasy made one of his select fifteen the Catalaunian Fields was, in fact, extraordinarily indecisive. There can be no doubt about the outcome of most of the other battles chosen by Creasy, for example his first and last, which were Marathon and Waterloo. But who really won on the Catalaunian Fields? Both Attila and Aetius, together with most of their followers, lived to fight another day. The Visigoths retired before the final outcome was known.

Attila, it is true, was prevented from advancing further and, in this respect, suffered an unfamiliar setback. But how great was the peril that the Roman Empire would have faced if Attila had won a clear victory on the Catalaunian Fields?

To answer this with certainty we must know what Attila's intentions really were when he invaded Gaul. On the face of it, to attack an empire, whose capital had recently been moved from Milan to Ravenna, by advancing up the Danube and the Rhine towards north-eastern France must seem a curious procedure. It is true that Attila counted on receiving reinforcements of Franks and Burgundians by taking this route, but this is hardly an adequate explanation.

Honoria's proposal of marriage and Attila's demand of half the Western Empire as a dowry have been assumed to account for Attila's conduct. One latter-day student of ancient Hun society has, it is true, dismissed the Honoria incident as a melodramatic story with 'all the earmarks of Byzantine court gossip.'[7] But even if the story is accepted – and there is no clear reason to doubt it – we still do not know quite why Attila found himself in mid-summer 451 in the vicinity of Orléans.

The reasons for Alaric's intrusions into various parts of the Roman Empire are clear, for he made no secret of them. He was looking for a land where his people could settle, a land which his successors found in southern France and northern Spain. The Vandals had similar aims, and they duly settled in North Africa.

Attila's campaigns were different. His people already had their home. Once they ceased to be nomads they settled in Hungary, and to Hungary they regularly returned. They returned from the vicinity of Constantinople, and they returned from France.

Can we then be sure that Attila was really threatening the overthrow and destruction of the Roman Empire and of all it stood for, and that he was prevented from achieving his ambitions only by a military setback near Châlons? Or is it possible that he was conducting one of his regular summer campaigns in search of the plunder needed to sustain his local economy? If this latter explanation is accepted it can be assumed that, after victory, he would have advanced at least as far as Toulouse and obtained what he wanted in the form of plunder and tribute from the Visigoth Kingdom.

It is also possible that during his long and successful advance through Germany and France Attila began to see opening up new prospects of conquest on a greater scale than anything he or his Hun predecessors had achieved.

A consideration of his conduct in the year following the battle of the Catalaunian Fields may help in providing answers to these questions.

CHAPTER 19

INVASION OF ITALY

Attila was astonished that Aetius had failed to exploit the advantage he had gained and that fighting had suddenly stopped. At first he believed that the sudden retreat of the Goths was a stratagem intended to lure him into an injudicious attack.

He remained immobilized for some time in the defensive position he had taken up. Then, when no action followed, he began to withdraw. Presumably, like Aetius, he had decided he could not be certain of victory, even after the Visigoths had departed.

The return journey to Hungary then began, probably by a somewhat different route, for Attila was reported to have been guided as far as the Rhine by Bishop Saint Loup. Saint Loup may still have been a prisoner and travelled unwillingly. Alternatively he may, like Orestes and Onegesius, have been yet another of the cultured men from the West who for one reason or another agreed to serve Attila.

According to Gregory of Tours, further atrocities were committed by the returning army, but for these he blamed neither the Huns nor others who remained under Attila's command, but some of his Germanic allies who followed in his wake, Thuringians in particular. Their deeds inspired one of Gibbon's peculiarly rich passages:

'They massacred their hostages as well as their captives; two hundred young maidens were tortured with exquisite and unrelenting rage; their bodies were torn asunder by wild horses, or their bones were crushed under the weight of rolling waggons; and their unburied limbs were abandoned on the public roads as a prey to dogs.' He concluded: 'Such were those savage ancestors whose imaginary virtues have sometimes excited the praise and envy of civilized ages!'

The French campaign may well have been a disappointment to Attila, not only in terms of territory won or lost, but in the quantity of the spoils of war which his army brought back. Almost immediately after his return to Hungary he was making further demands for large quantities of gold, and doing so without being in a position to back his demands by adequate force.

The gold he demanded was the annual tribute that he had been able to rely on receiving from the Eastern Empire – more often than not – so long as Theodosius II was alive.

Theodosius's successor, Marcian, though regarded at first as little more than the nominee – albeit also husband – of the powerful Pulcheria, had begun to exhibit both strength and statesmanship. He refrained from attacking Attila's kingdom when it was weakened by the despatch of the army to the West. (In the event he waited for further changes in relative strengths before entering into a decisive military engagement with the Huns.) But he had no intention of giving Attila any more gold.

He did send an embassy under the command of a military leader named Apollonius to discuss relations in general, but when Attila learned that he was not to receive any tribute he refused to let Apollonius cross the Danube. He also threatened war, but evidently came to the conclusion that it might be a rash move.[1] Instead he decided on a new campaign, which he must have been considering for some time. This was an invasion of Italy.

To invade Italy was a logical consequence of demanding half the Western Empire as Honoria's dowry. It may also have been planned as a means of fulfilling Attila's greatest ambition. Among serious students today of the life of Attila, and of the world in which he lived, are some who are convinced that his ambition was to conquer the world much as Alexander had once done.[2]

Their arguments are plausible, and if they are right, the capture of Rome would have been seen as a necessary preliminary step on the way to even greater achievements. Alaric had captured Rome some forty years earlier, and one who saw himself as an even greater conqueror could hardly be content with doing less.

It can also be argued that, having partially failed in France, and doubting his capacity to succeed in the Balkans, Attila decided that Italy would provide him with the most readily available source of the plunder he needed to sustain his economy. He may well have learnt that Aetius, after returning across the Alps, had been able to retain only a comparatively small part of the force with which he had set out.[3]

Whatever his motives may have been, Attila set off for northern Italy early in the spring of 452, once again commanding an international force, which included a variety of Germanic peoples. No details are known of the route, but it was probably similar to that taken, in reverse, by the British Eighth Army in 1945 on its way to occupy parts of Austria, that is to say through the Klagenfurt gap and on a line roughly parallel with, and near to, the present border between Italy and Slovenia. Alaric had earlier taken much the same route.

The army moved in the direction of where Trieste stands today, but was halted at Aquileia, a place with a remarkable history. Once a fortified town of major importance, it is today no more than a village, a transformation for which Attila was to a considerable extent responsible.

Aquileia is situated, a little inland, at the head of the Adriatic, a few kilometres to the west of Trieste. It was founded by the Romans for the very purpose to which it was put when first Alaric, and then Attila, confronted it, that is to say to prevent the irruption into Italy of barbarians who had crossed the Julian Alps.

At first merely a fortress, it became before long an important commercial as well as military centre and was stated by Ausonius to be the fourth greatest city in Italy, following Rome, Milan and Capua. Augustus took up residence in Aquileia for a time, and it was there that he received Herod the Great in 10 BC. It became the capital of Venetia and had the distinction at one time of being the only city in Italy, other than Rome, that had the right to strike coins.

Whoever held Aquileia was likely to command much of northern Italy. One of the great Roman roads, the Postumian way, ended there, but smaller, though excellent, roads led from it to such outposts of empire as Noricum and Pannonia.

Until the arrival of Attila's army, Aquileia had remained impregnable.

Alaric and his mass following of women and children seem to have bypassed the city, but Attila decided to lay siege to it.

What followed was something new in Attila's experience. He had accepted early in his military career that he could not attack Constantinople successfully, and he had refrained from trying. Orléans had provided unexpected resistance, but, had it not been for the sudden arrival of a relieving army, he would almost certainly have taken it after a comparatively short siege. Aquileia continued to resist for month after month.

With every week that passed the prospects for a successful campaign in Italy deteriorated. Italy is a country designed by nature, even more than most, for summer rather than winter campaigning. In 1944, while in southern Italy, Field Marshal Montgomery wrote in a letter to one of his subordinate commanders: 'I do not think we can conduct a winter campaign in this country. If I remember right Caesar used to go into winter quarters – a very sound thing to do.' He added two exclamation marks.[4] For Attila, with large numbers of men and horses to feed on what he could obtain from the countryside, the problems of winter campaigning would have been vastly greater.

At the end of three months, with no indication that the garrison of Aquileia was considering either surrendering or abandoning the city, Attila was on the point of giving up the siege. The logical consequence of this would have been to call off his Italian campaign, perhaps postponing it until the following year, perhaps abandoning it altogether.

The decision he finally took was believed to have been brought about by a curious incident, which was vividly described by Procopius among others.

'While Attila was besieging Aquileia,' Procopius wrote, 'they tell the story that the following good fortune befell him. When he was able to capture the place neither by force nor by any other means, he gave up the siege in despair and commanded the whole army without any delay to make their preparations for departure, in order that on the morrow all might move from there at sunrise.

'The following day about sunrise the barbarians had raised the siege and were already beginning their departure when a single male stork, which had a nest on a certain tower of the city wall and was rearing its nestlings there, suddenly rose and left the place with his young. The father stork was flying, but the little storks, since they were not yet quite ready to fly, were at times sharing their father's flight and at times riding on his back, and thus they flew off and went away from the city.

'When Attila saw this (for he was most clever at comprehending and interpreting all things) he commanded the army, they say, to remain still in the same place, adding that the bird would never have gone flying off at random from there with his nestlings, unless he was prophesying that some evil would come to the place at no distant time.

'Thus, they say, the army of the barbarians settled down to the siege once more, and not long after that a portion of that wall – the very part which held the nest of that bird – for no apparent reason fell down, and it became possible for the enemy to enter the city at that point, and thus Aquileia was captured by storm.'

Procopius ended his account: 'Such is the story touching Aquileia.' Others have attributed the interpretation of the meaning of the storks' flight to the priests who always accompanied Attila, and point to this as an example of the importance of the faith he professed in determining Attila's actions.[5]

The destruction inflicted on Aquileia by Attila's army was total, and it never again became a city of major importance. Some rebuilding was done, but rather more than a century after the passage of Attila's army Aquileia was again sacked and destroyed by the Lombards. After that even the bishopric was transferred to Grado and the civil administration to Venice. The culminating disaster was an earthquake in the fifteenth century. By the late twentieth century the great city which had once defied Attila had become a village of a few thousand inhabitants, rich in mosaics and intriguing in the excavations that continued to be conducted.[6]

The wholesale destruction of a major town early in a campaign was a strategy adopted by Attila in both France and Germany. Metz recovered to become a city of importance. Aquileia did not. But the news of what had happened in both places spread, as it was no doubt intended to, and the rulers of other cities duly took note.

The destruction of cities for exemplary purposes was already by Attila's day a long-established practice. No people engaged in it more ruthlessly and effectively than the Romans of the republican era when they destroyed Carthage in its entirety. Attila was carrying on an established tradition, and he did so to some effect.

The length of the siege of Aquileia delayed his campaign far longer than he can have wished. The news of the city's destruction was to have the opposite effect.

CHAPTER 20

THE CITIES OF LOMBARDY FALL

After the capture of Aquileia, Attila's army advanced westward, taking advantage of flat and fertile territory and, after a time, following the line of the river Po.

If, as has been suggested, Attila conceived his Italian campaign primarily as a march on Rome, it might be thought that he chose a surprising route, for not until he had passed Milan did he begin to move south in the direction of Pavia. Certainly his route shows that he had no intention of capturing Ravenna, then the capital of the Western Empire.

As a way of advancing from one rich city to another, while taking advantage of the contours of the land, Attila's route was admirably chosen. No doubt he also had to take into consideration the whereabouts of any army that might oppose him. Of this all that is known is that Aetius had lost the support of the Alans, as well as that of the Visigoths, and that he had returned to Italy with a sadly diminished force. The consistent refusal of Roman citizens to man their own armies in adequate numbers was having a disastrous effect.

From Aquileia the army moved west and a little south to Padua. This was an important city, supported by thriving agriculture and industry, and was reputed to have no fewer than five hundred citizens of equestrian rank.[1] Attila's forces plundered it thoroughly, but before their arrival an appreciable number of citizens deemed it prudent to escape. According to a long-established tradition, it was these refugees, fleeing from Attila, who founded the city of Venice.

Gibbon, drawing primarily on Cassiodorus, whose duties as a sixth-century prefect may well have included administration of the Venice area, but also on later Italian historians, wrote: 'Many families of

Aquileia, Padua and the adjacent towns, who fled from the sword of the Huns, found a safe, though obscure, refuge in the neighbouring islands. At the extremity of the Gulf, where the Hadriatic feebly imitates the tides of the ocean, near an hundred small islands are separated by shallow water from the continent, and protected from the waves by several long slips of land, which admit the entrance of vessels through some secret and narrow channels.

'Till the middle of the fifth century these remote and sequestered spots remained without cultivation, with few inhabitants, and almost without a name. But the manners of the Venetian fugitives, their arts and their government, were gradually formed by their new situation.' Cassiodorus, no less colourfully, likened the first settlers in Venice to waterfowl that had fixed their nests on the waves.

Later research has provided evidence of human habitation in Venice long before the fifth century, but the earlier dwellers seem to have lived largely in poverty, depending for their livelihood on fishing. Refugees from the mainland, some from the Huns, others, later, from the Lombards, almost certainly played a major part in developing the twelve townships in the lagoon which eventually formed the city, then the republic of Venice. For a long time these lagoon townships continued to be administered from Padua.

Vicenza and Verona were the next towns on Attila's route. The beautiful city of Vicenza that we associate with Andrea Palladio was not, under the Roman Empire, a place of major importance, but Verona was. No other city in northern Italy has Roman remains comparable in magnificence with its huge first-century amphitheatre and other structures. Among the city's administrative responsibilities was the collection of the inheritance tax from all of Italy north of the Po. For this and kindred reasons the plunder available to Attila's army in Verona must have been substantial.[2]

The poet Catullus was born in Verona, and he must frequently have taken the road from there to Sirmione, the spa on the shore of Lake Garda, where he had a villa, in which he wrote many of his poems to his mistress Lesbia. (In spite of the frequent complaints in his verses of poverty he had more than one such villa.)

Attila's soldiers also took this road, and as they advanced, seeing, on the right-hand side, the long stretch of Lake Garda with mountains in the background, they may well have felt deeply content. Not only were they unopposed by any hostile army, but they increasingly found that the gates of cities were opened to let them in. They were not so much made welcome as recognized to be a force that it would be unwise to resist. Brescia and Bergamo were taken without difficulty, and the way was open to the former imperial capital, Milan.

No resistance to Attila was organized by the Emperor Valentinian III in Ravenna. Aetius was in favour of military action, in spite of the reduced strength of his army, and he continued to show considerable fortitude as the danger from Attila's army grew. Valentinian was not to be persuaded.

Valentinian evidently disliked Aetius. His mother, Galla Placidia, may have passed on her distrust of him. He may have resented and feared Aetius's growing authority. His antipathy may have been wholly unreasonable, as his subsequent conduct suggests. But whatever the reasons, having turned down Aetius's military plans, he left Ravenna for Rome.

Valentinian's departure from Ravenna has been described as an ignominious flight, but this assumption is open to question. He was in no danger from Attila in Ravenna. Indeed, he seemed much more likely to encounter danger by going to Rome. In assessing his motives it is also necessary to take account of the prejudices harboured by early chroniclers ever since the rather preposterous story was put about that Galla Placidia deliberately brought him up to be depraved.

There were few options open to him. The Empire, which had recovered some strength under Galla Placidia's guidance, was now tottering. Visigoths and Vandals had established functioning kingdoms in large areas that had once been indisputably part of the Roman Empire. Ostrogoths, Alans and others could provide military support to Rome or withdraw it much as they saw fit. The kind of assistance from the Eastern Empire which had helped to sustain Honorius, and which Valentinian himself had received when fighting the Vandals, was no longer forthcoming. On top of all this, in the last fifteen months a large army commanded by a man of such compelling magnetism as Attila had roamed at will through much of Germany, France and now Italy.

Valentinian was not a defeatist. When Theodosius II had advocated accepting Attila's terms in the matter of Honoria's dowry he had resisted. Though an unattractive character and a cruel one, he was capable of sound reasoning, as a number of his public statements show.

In one of these he declared: 'It is a pronouncement worthy of the majesty of the ruler that the Emperor should declare himself bound by the laws, so much does our authority depend on the authority of the law. To submit our imperial office to the laws is in truth a greater thing than our imperial sovereignty.'[3]

He was also, like his mother, a dedicated Christian. Sometimes his faith led him in the direction of persecution and censorship. In the third century the Greek Neoplatonist Porphyry had written a work entitled *Against the Christians*. Eunapius described it as 'the most serious and thorough document, as well the fairest, in which Christianity has ever been attacked, and free from the scorn and bitterness of Julian's work of the same name.' Valentinian ordered all fifteen volumes to be destroyed. Only fragments remain.

In some respects his thinking was close to that of Pope Leo I, by whom he was strongly influenced, and in one of his decrees he pronounced that 'the bishops of Gaul or any other province should take no decision contrary to the ancient rules of discipline without the consent and authority of the venerable Pope of the eternal city.'[4]

In the light of this evidence and of what actually happened, it seems probable that Valentinian left Ravenna for Rome, not in precipitate flight, but in the hope of finding some effective means of resisting Attila.

Meanwhile Attila's advance continued. His troops reached the ancient city of Mediolanum, later to be known as Milano, the fourth-century capital of the Western Roman Empire, where the Emperor Constantine had pronounced his famous edict officially recognizing the Christian religion. No resistance was offered. Attila briefly occupied the royal palace, where he was reported to have asserted his power over Rome in an ingenious manner.

His attention was called to a picture in which Caesars were depicted sitting on thrones with Scythian princes prostrate at their feet. The painter was brought to Attila and instructed to make appropriate changes. Roman Emperors were now to be shown as suppliants emptying bags of gold tribute before the throne of a monarch, presumably Attila himself.[5] Unfortunately no such picture has survived.

A pictorial representation of Attila is however to be seen in the next city in the line of his advance. This was Pavia, then known as Ticinum. Here in the Charterhouse there are sixty reliefs in the form of medallions portraying heroes of antiquity or of the Bible. Among them is Attila. He has been given a striking face, even though his features are quite unlike those described by Priscus. He has an aquiline nose and the appearance rather of a Roman senator or general.

After it left Pavia, Attila's army seems to have advanced in a somewhat haphazard manner. It was certainly not moving in the direction of Rome, for it was next reported to be still in Lombardy, well to the east of Pavia, on the banks of the small river Mincio, and not far from Mantua.

Here there was to be an historic encounter. In France bishops and abbots, some of them canonized, had interceded with Attila, asking him to spare their cities. In Italy, on the river Mincio, he was to be confronted by the Pope himself.

CHAPTER 21

ATTILA AND THE POPE

Leo I was one of the two Popes on whom the Catholic Church conferred the title 'the Great'. The other was Gregory I, who lived in the sixth century.[1] Leo's papacy extended over twenty-one years, beginning in 440, when he succeeded an undistinguished figure, Xystus II.

It was a period in which, while the Western Empire declined, the Church in the West grew both in strength and cohesion. That it did so was attributable, to a considerable extent, to Leo's personality, faith and administrative skills. A little more than half-way through his papacy Leo had his meeting with Attila.

To Leo the Empire was an institution of great spiritual, as well as material, importance. In writing of God's condescension expressed in the incarnation of His son he stated: 'That the consequences of this unspeakable generosity might be made known throughout the whole world divine providence fashioned the Roman Empire, the growth of which was extended to boundaries so wide that all races everywhere became next-door neighbours.'

Leo was continually conscious of his status and responsibilities as the successor of St Peter, in whose name and on whose behalf he exercised his authority. Theologians have even accused him of rewriting history by exaggerating the contribution of St Peter, and diminishing that of St Paul, in the early history of the Church. It was also said of him that when he preached or wrote a letter he believed that it was St Peter speaking or guiding his pen.[2]

One of the many tasks he set himself was to improve the quality of the priesthood, members of whom, he was disturbed to find, were engaging in the prohibited practice of usury. This led him to ban the ordination of all those who were required to undertake some form of hereditary labour on the ground that men in the service of God must be free from other obligations.

He was an authoritarian, who did not condone dissent, and Valentinian's action in calling upon bishops in Gaul to submit to papal authority was no doubt inspired by him. In the same spirit, while not an active heresy-hunter, he made it clear that he would not tolerate within the Church the heresy of Manicheeism.

Manicheeism was a belief strongly influenced by Eastern philosophy and faith, in particular Zoroastranism. Among its concepts was a dualism of light and darkness, of spirit and matter. This led to a ready association of the material world with evil. A natural consequence was the adoption of extreme forms of asceticism and renunciation of worldly things.[3]

The Manichees with whom Pope Leo seems to have been primarily concerned went even further. Sexual intercourse for purposes of procreation was wrong, they believed, on the curious ground that in the reproductive process light was imprisoned. One way of avoiding this was total abstention. Another was sexual activity between men. This Pope Leo did not favour.

He was a firm upholder of the sanctity of Christian marriage. In an age in which large numbers of men were taken captive by the various barbarian armies, their wives, having assumed them to be dead, frequently remarried. Occasionally the husbands returned, and when called upon to pronounce on such happenings, Pope Leo declared that the rights of the first husband must be respected, and that if the woman continued to live with the second husband she was to be excommunicated.

In this and in other pronouncements Pope Leo made it clear that it was only the Christian form of marriage with which he was concerned. Different rules applied to a man's relations with a concubine. Indeed, he stated that if a priest had given his daughter – priests did at that time have daughters – to a man who had a concubine, it was not to be taken that he had given his daughter to a married man.[4]

Leo I was not a great theologian. Profound theology was still largely the preserve of the Eastern Church, in which scholars could assemble the combined benefits of the Christian gospel, Greek philosophy and

Eastern mysticism. His strengths lay in being an excellent administrator, an inspiring preacher and a man of balanced judgement.

He had a clear idea of the direction in which his followers should be led and of the diversions and wrong turnings to be avoided. He was much respected by his contemporaries in the civil administration of Rome, and it was for this, among other reasons, that they called upon him to confront Attila face to face.

The meeting that took place on the banks of the Mincio, a river that enchanted Dante, in the summer of 452 gave rise to at least one artistic masterpiece and a great deal of speculation. The known facts are few.

The delegation sent to Attila from Rome consisted of three men. Two of them were leading senators. One, Trigetius, the Prefect of Rome, was an experienced negotiator who had reached an agreement more than fifteen years earlier with the Vandal King Geiseric in Africa. The other, Gennadius Avienus, a rich and successful politician, held a responsible post concerned with Rome's water supplies. In diplomatic standing Pope Leo may well have been only the third of the delegation's members.

Their task was to persuade Attila not to attack Rome. How they did so and what happened at the meeting is a tale that has been much repeated and much embroidered.

Attila was reported to have received the delegates while lying at ease in his tent. He would certainly not have been overawed by their presence. They were the suppliants, not he.

According to the accounts of later chroniclers, Attila was deeply impressed by the eloquence of Pope Leo, by his pontifical robes and by his majestic aspect. The climax came when St Peter and St Paul appeared alongside the Pope and threatened Attila with instant death unless he acceded to the Pope's request.

It is this picture of St Peter and St Paul with Pope Leo and Attila which was handed down to posterity through the genius of Raphael of Urbino. In it both the Pope and Attila are on horseback.

In his short life of thirty-seven years Raphael, in addition to his huge output as a painter and being chosen as chief architect of St Peter's, developed a keen interest in the past. This led to his appointment as commissioner of antiquities in Rome, a post in which he advocated the excavation of the Forum and tried vainly to stop the destruction of the Appian Way.[5]

Several rooms above the Borgia apartments in the Vatican Palace were already decorated with frescoes, but Pope Julius II, deeming them to be old-fashioned, instructed Raphael to paint over them. As an antiquarian Raphael deplored the proposal. As an artist he accepted the commission.

One of the frescoes he produced in this way was known as 'The Repulse of Attila'. It was begun in Julius II's lifetime and finished in that of his successor. A consequence of this was that the face of the successor, Pope Leo X, appears twice in the painting, once as a cardinal riding behind the central figure of the Pope, and once as Pope Leo I himself.

In the next century the baroque sculptor Alessandro Algardi, who delighted in portraying violent action, chose the same theme for a relief executed for St Peter's in Rome. In this too the Pope, with divine help, is shown triumphing over the retreating barbarian. The principal figures are more than three metres in height.

Through the work of these masters countless people through the ages must have held a picture in their memory of Attila being repulsed by divine intervention, many no doubt assuming that the incident occurred when Attila was on the point of capturing Rome. Even the sceptical Gibbon described the apparition of St Peter and St Paul as 'one of the noblest legends of ecclesiastical tradition.'

Rationalists will almost certainly conclude that through the passage of time and people's credulity the figures of the saints were substituted for those of the two senators, Trigetius and Avienus. This may indeed have been so, and to what extent, if any, Attila was influenced by the personality of Pope Leo and the prestige of the office he held can only be guessed at.

The accounts given by early historians certainly suggest that religion, and not only the Christian religion, played an important part in deciding events. In this, as so often, Priscus, and then Jordanes, led where others, including modern commentators, have followed.

'Attila's mind', Jordanes wrote, 'had been bent on going to Rome. But his followers, as the historian Priscus relates, took him away, not out of regard for the city to which they were hostile, but because they remembered the case of Alaric, the former king of the Visigoths. They distrusted the good fortune of their own king, inasmuch as Alaric did not live long after the sack of Rome, but straightway departed this life. Therefore while Attila's spirit was wavering between going and not going, and he still lingered to ponder the matter, an embassy came to him from Rome to seek peace.'

The mere fact that Alaric died soon after capturing Rome would certainly not have been enough to persuade Attila to halt his advance. But it is not impossible that Attila's priests foretold disaster if he continued, and that the fate of Alaric was cited as an example of what might happen. If it was true that he adopted a defensive strategy on the Catalaunian Fields after defeat had been foretold, and that he continued the siege of Aquileia also through supernatural guidance, he could have been deterred by soothsayers from capturing Rome.

Any such explanation must be speculation. What is known is that Attila did turn back after the meeting on the banks of the Mincio and Rome was spared.

Modern historians tend to attribute this, not so much to the embassy in which Pope Leo took part, as to economic conditions. A famine did occur in Italy in the winter of 450–51 and it is possible that its effects were still being felt in the summer of 452.[6]

Armies invading Italy have more than once suffered from shortage of food, polluted water and heat. An account has survived of the experiences of Frankish invaders in 540, who were unable to obtain any provisions except cattle and the waters of the Po. Most of them were attacked by diarrhoea and dysentery, which they were unable to shake off. A third of the Frankish army was reported to have died from these causes.[7]

During Attila's campaign shortage of food was believed to have been accompanied by some form of plague, which may well have been malaria. Nothing being known of the cause of this disease, its incidence in the Roman Empire was, understandably, not reported with any accuracy, but it was almost certainly widespread. Indeed, some historians have even been of the opinion that among the principal causes of the collapse of the Empire in the West were malaria and deforestation.

It has also been suggested, on good authority, that there were compelling military reasons for Attila to abandon his campaign. While Attila's army was in Italy the Emperor Mercian sent a military force across the Danube. He also provided Aetius with reinforcements. With the prospect of a war on two fronts Attila may well have felt that his only safe course was to retreat.

The explanations as to why Attila never reached Rome have indeed been many. Divine intervention, the personality of Pope Leo I, the forebodings of soothsayers, food shortages, pestilence, and a military threat from the Empire in the East have been among them.

There is yet another possible explanation, to which little, if any, attention has hitherto been paid. This is that Attila had achieved all he could have hoped for in the year 452, and that he decided the time had come to follow his normal practice and return to Hungary before winter set in.

In 451 he had fought the battle of the Catalaunian Fields in June. Not long afterwards he had begun his protracted homeward journey. In 452 he brought an army over mountains, presumably late enough in the spring for much of the snow to have melted, was delayed for three months outside Aquileia, and afterwards captured a series of cities in Lombardy. All this being so, the meeting with the Pope and the two senators could hardly have taken place before the autumn, by which time the campaigning season would be nearing its end.

One account of the meeting by the river Mincio mentions payment of the dowry once demanded by Attila.[8] Another tells of threats to Italy uttered by Attila unless he obtained what he wanted.[9] From these it is reasonable to conclude that Attila both demanded and received payment of gold, as had happened in the past when he threatened Constantinople.

There is also evidence in the correspondence of Pope Symmachus, who was confirmed in office after his election in 498 by Theodoric, that Pope Leo had negotiated with Attila for the release of prisoners, not only Christians, but also Jews and pagans. If, as was implied, he succeeded, Attila no doubt received substantial ransom money. With all these negotiations completed he could well have considered his mission for the year 452 successfully accomplished.

Pope Leo, Trigetius and Avienus clearly achieved what they wanted, but so, it is quite reasonable to suppose, did Attila. He may indeed have had no intention of advancing further than the river Mincio, where he was no nearer Rome than he had been at Pavia.

CHAPTER 22

THE WEDDING NIGHT AND AFTER

The threat to Attila's kingdom by the Emperor Marcian was a real one. Exactly how Attila planned to resist it is not known, nor can we be certain of the route he took on leaving Italy. Jordanes wrote: 'Attila returned to his own country, seeming to regret the peace and to be vexed at the cessation of war. For he sent ambassadors to Marcian, Emperor of the East, threatening to devastate the provinces because that which had been promised to him by Theodosius, a former Emperor, was in no wise performed, and saying that he would show himself more cruel to his foes than ever.'

From this we may conclude that Attila was planning some kind of offensive, possibly similar to those that had been conducted in the reign of Theodosius. But a curious account of his actions follows.

'As he was shrewd and crafty, he threatened in one direction and moved his army in another, for in the midst of these preparations he turned his face towards the Visigoths, who had yet to feel his vengeance. Hastening back by a different way than before, he decided to reduce that part of the Alani which was settled across the river Loire, in order that by attacking them, and thus changing the aspect of war, he might become a more terrible menace to the Visigoths.'

If Jordanes is to be believed, Attila's army must have been extraordinarily mobile during the winter of 452–53, for Jordanes goes on to state that for his new campaign Attila set out from Dacia and Pannonia.

There follows an account of a battle that other historians have chosen to ignore. Attila, Jordanes wrote, 'moved his array against the Alani. But Thorismund, King of the Visigoths, with like quickness of thought, perceived Attila's trick. By forced marches he came to the Alani before him and was well prepared to check the advance of Attila when he came after him. They joined battle in almost the same way as before at the Catalaunian Plains, and Thorismund dashed his hopes of victory, for he routed him and drove him from the land without a triumph, compelling him to flee to his own country.'

Jordanes from time to time indulged in fantasy, and he was not above attributing triumphs to Gothic peoples which never happened. But, in the absence of contemporary historians, other than Priscus, whose works have survived, he is one of the principal sources of posterity's knowledge of Attila. It is therefore dangerous to overlook anything he wrote, but it is difficult to suggest a time when this otherwise unrecorded battle might have taken place. Attila was certainly in Hungary in the spring of 453, as we know from events recorded as having taken place then.

Among his other activities was the taking of a new wife to add to the many he already had. Her name was Ildico, and she was described as young and beautiful. Nothing else is known of her for certain. The belief that she was a Burgundian rests on flimsy evidence.

The wedding, which was considered a major occasion for rejoicing, was celebrated in the wooden palace near the river Tisza, which Priscus had visited. Drinking went on through the evening, and Attila retired to bed late. His servants thought it wise not to disturb him too soon.

'On the following day,' Jordanes wrote, 'when a great part of the morning was spent, the royal attendants suspected some ill and, after a great uproar, broke in the doors. There they found the death of Attila accomplished by an effusion of blood, without any wound, and the girl with downcast face weeping beneath her veil.'

An artery was stated to have burst so that Attila, who was lying prone, was suffocated by a torrent of blood. Ildico was reported to have 'lamented her own danger'.

Attila's body was laid out under a silk pavilion in the middle of the plain. The most skilful horsemen, carefully chosen, galloped wildly round the body in order to gladden the heart of the dead leader. A hymn was sung, which has been translated from the original Hun words.[1]

It tells of Attila, the greatest of all Hun kings, son of Mundzuk, lord of the most heroic of peoples, who, with unprecedented might, ruled over Scythian and Germanic lands, filled both Roman Empires with fear, seized their cities and exacted annual tribute from them.

Attila's male followers cut off much of their hair and gashed their faces so that the great king should be lamented, not by the cries of women, but by the blood of warriors.

'In the secrecy of night,' Jordanes wrote, 'they buried his body in the earth. They bound his coffins, the first with gold, the second with silver, and the third with the strength of iron. They also added the arms of foemen won in the fight, trappings of rare worth, sparkling with gems, and ornaments of all sorts whereby princely state is maintained.'

Finally, 'that so great riches might be kept from human curiosity they slew those appointed to the work, a dreadful reward for their labour. Thus sudden death was the lot of those who buried him as well as of him who was buried.'

That Attila died of natural causes soon began to be disputed. By the sixth century the Byzantine chronicler Count Marcellinus was writing that he was murdered by the bride whom he had just married. It was a belief for which there was no supporting evidence.[2]

Attila's burial site is not known, although, as one distinguished archaeologist has pointed out, it has given rise to more speculation than any other burial site in the world with the possible exception of that of Alexander the Great.[3]

The same archaeologist is of the opinion that the body was almost certainly placed in a coffin together with costly treasures, and that the coffin was buried in the earth. For this reason, like anything else that has been buried, it may one day be discovered. But if it is, it can hardly be identified with any certainty – not least because no inscribed words can be expected – and the task of searching scientifically is too formidable to be undertaken seriously. At the very least the area between the rivers Tisza and Danube in which it might reasonably be found must measure some twenty thousand square kilometres.[4]

Nevertheless, hope of finding Attila's grave will probably never be abandoned. In Hungary the belief grew up that his body was buried in a river, either the Tisza or the Danube. This almost certainly derived from a confusion between Jordanes's accounts of the burials of Alaric and of Attila. But the belief will no doubt continue to be held.

Attila was sole King of the Huns for a mere eight years. In that short time the impact he made on his contemporaries was extraordinary. Much of this was due to his conquests. Eight years was a short period in which to hold both Eastern and Western Empires to ransom with the threat of capturing and destroying both Constantinople and Rome, in addition to overrunning much of Germany and France.

As a conqueror, however, his achievements were not unique, others surpassing him, both in territories overrun and, more importantly, in victories that endured. Alaric captured Rome, Attila did not. Athaulf the Visigoth, in France, and Geiseric the Vandal, in North Africa, carved out kingdoms which their peoples occupied for generations to come. Attila added no territory whatever to the kingdom that his predecessors had successfully enlarged.

Yet Attila was feared and, there can be little doubt, respected more than any of the other military leaders of his time or of the decades preceding it. This is to some extent to be explained by his race and his religion. Visigoths, Ostrogoths, Vandals, Franks and others were predominantly Christians and, with the liberal policy adopted in the Empire, liable to be Roman citizens. As such they may not have been liked, but they were accepted by educated Romans as being capable of outstanding achievements.

Attila was neither a Christian nor a Roman citizen, and his people were regarded as alien, crude and frightening. This must have made the fact that men of so many races enlisted under Attila's command and served him so loyally even more impressive. Nor could the deference that the kings and other leaders of these people showed to Attila have been overlooked. Jordanes clearly had grounds for stating that they 'hung upon Attila's nod like slaves.'

Moreover, there is no evidence to suggest that there were any desertions from Attila's ranks. Aetius was a successful commander and a skilful diplomat, and he was acknowledged as a natural leader of men. Yet his armies were certainly not free from desertions, even though he had the authority of the Roman Empire behind him, whereas Attila had to depend on his own personality and reputation.

Much in Attila's achievements and personality may have seemed paradoxical to his contemporaries. Priscus knew him personally, and his is the only unquestionably authentic account we have of Attila's way of life. The portrait he presents is of a man of dignity and compassion, modest in his personal habits and requirements, holding a court that attracted thoughtful men of a variety of nations.

At much the same time as Priscus was writing, the sophisticated and well-informed St Jerome, churchman of authority, was writing of the Huns in much the same way as he wrote of cannibals who considered the buttocks of shepherds to be delicacies.

Whether Attila was either a great ruler and/or a great military commander is clearly debatable. Jordanes had no doubt. 'Attila', he wrote, 'was lord over all the Huns and almost the sole earthly ruler of all the tribes of Scythia, a man marvellous for his glorious fame among all nations.' Modern commentators tend to be more sceptical.

A British historian of Marxist leanings has belittled Attila as a military leader for 'succumbing to the courage of a free peasantry' on the Catalaunian Fields.[5] Modern Hungarian authorities, more pertinently, make the point that it was Attila's immediate predecessors, rather than he himself, who raised the kingdom of the Huns to the level at which it could deal with the Roman Empire as a sovereign state to be respected and feared.[6] On the other hand, one of these authorities has pointed out, had Attila lived longer he might well have successfully attacked the Eastern Empire, in which event much of history would have been changed.[7]

All verdicts on Attila's achievements must be based on an understanding or, at least, an assumption of what his aims were. If he sought to enlarge the kingdom of the Huns, he was clearly a failure. If he hoped to conquer most of the civilized world, it could be said that he was not granted enough time. But if, having consolidated the Hun kingdom – his greatest achievement, in Mommsen's judgement – he simply devised a method of enriching its economy by a series of long-distance raids, he may be adjudged a considerable benefactor of his nation.

No judgement of Attila can be complete which is based solely on his achievements or, indeed, on what took place in his lifetime. For appreciation of his full stature – it is surely difficult to avoid the word 'greatness' – there is more to be taken into account. We must consider first what happened in his kingdom, and in the territories where he fought, immediately after his death. After that we must turn to Attila the legend, which in some respects is even more extraordinary than Attila the man.

CHAPTER 23

THE SONS OF ATTILA

For some eight years Attila had been sole ruler of the Huns in a manner that was unique in the history of his people. Soon after his death there was a partial reversion to an older system. Attila's eldest son, Ellak, by a wife named Arykan, became King. He had the support of Onegesius, Attila's principal administrator, whom he regarded as his friend. Onegesius had played a leading part in ensuring the smooth running of Attila's system of absolute control, and it is reasonable to assume that he looked forward to a continuation of it.

Ellak's two brothers had other ideas. One was named Dengizik. The other, Ernak, was known to have been Attila's favourite and was presumably the boy on whom Attila had looked with such affection in Priscus's presence. These two younger sons hoped for the kind of division of power that had been the practice when Attila was a subordinate prince under Bleda.

To some extent their wishes were met. There was no division of territory, but a division of rule of a kind that Attila would never have countenanced, and which indicated the persistence of the type of thinking that prevailed when the Huns had been a nomadic people. Instead of territory, Dengizik and Ernak were given control over some of the subordinate peoples who tilled the land, served as soldiers or otherwise did the bidding of Hun rulers.

In this division of rule the Huns failed to take into account the new strength which some of the subordinate peoples had acquired, particularly when campaigning under Attila's command. The very fact of division was also a virtual guarantee of instability.

Within a year of Attila's death fighting broke out in the lower Danube area between factions supporting the different brothers. In this Ellak was successful, and the two younger brothers had to make their escape from Hun territory.

On returning north after dealing with this disturbance Ellak was confronted with a much more serious challenge to his rule. This came from Ardaric, King of the Gepids, Attila's most reliable ally, who had supported him on his assumption of power after Bleda's death, and had provided him with important military contingents on his foreign campaigns.

Ardaric had decided to rebel against Hun rule and, in doing so, received the support – or at least the encouragement – of the Emperor Marcian. A battle was fought in 454, or possibly 455, in Pannonia near a river called Nedao, in which the Huns were opposed by a combined force of Gepids and a variety of Germanic and Iranian peoples.

The battle of the Nedao river was far more decisive than that of the Catalaunian Fields in determining the future of the Hun people. Ardaric's forces gained an overwhelming victory. Ellak himself was killed, and the defeat the Huns suffered was the beginning of the end of their empire.

The immediate inheritors of the Hun Empire – in particular that part of Hungary between the Danube and the Tisza, where their capital was situated – were the Gepids, whom the Huns had regarded as tillers of their soil.

Another consequence of the defeat of the Huns was a consolidation of the power of the Emperor Marcian, whose diplomacy had contributed effectively to the Hun defeat. Territory was reallocated in accordance with his wishes, and the Eastern Empire was freed for a time from the kind of attack to which it had been continually subject since the Huns became a major power. Marcian made a formal alliance with the Ostrogoths, assigning them territory in northern Pannonia. Other peoples, including Skirians and Heruls, were settled further to the east.

The Gepids were confirmed in possession of the territory they occupied, but their period of ascendancy was a brief one. They were defeated by Ostrogoths in a major battle in 469. Other unsuccessful battle followed against the same people, with forced migrations as a consequence. Eventually the Gepids were driven as far away as Provence, where they were assigned the task of protecting the Ostrogoth Empire against Burgundian attacks.[1]

While the Gepids were enjoying their brief supremacy, Dengizik, Ernak and their Hun followers were driven towards the lower reaches of the Danube. They hoped to establish a permanent home there, and in 466 they sent an embassy to the Emperor Leo I, who in 457 had succeeded Marcian.

Leo was a military man, one of the many emperors who owed his elevation to the army, although he seems to have been the first to be crowned in a formal ceremony by the Patriarch of Constantinople. He was served by some ambitious generals. One of them, Anthemius, even commanded an expedition of more than a thousand ships and a hundred thousand men against the Vandals in Africa, albeit unsuccessfully.

The Hun embassy, after apologizing for damage inflicted in the past, pleaded for the creation of a market at an agreed point on the Danube, where citizens of the Empire and Huns could exchange goods. This was the kind of arrangement which had been found satisfactory – indeed, from the Hun point of view, economically necessary – in the past. To Leo and the kind of military adviser to whom he looked for guidance the proposal was of little interest, and the Hun embassy returned to report its failure.

Dengizik's response was in accordance with Hun tradition. He decided on war and in the winter of 466–67 he led an army across the frozen Danube. Ignoring the local imperial military commander, Anagestes, who was the son of Arnegliscus, Attila's former opponent, he sent another embassy to the Emperor Leo.

Adopting the tone of his father, Dengizik demanded land for himself and his army on payment of an annual rent, stating that the alternative was war. The request was refused and obedience to imperial rule demanded.

In the fighting that followed, Dengizik's forces resisted those of Anthemius for some two years. Then, in 469, after Anagestes took over, the Huns suffered total defeat. In Constantinople victory was celebrated by publicly displaying Dengizik's skull as an act of revenge for the damage that his father had inflicted on the Empire.

Ernak acted more cautiously. Faced by the prospect of attack by

Bulgar and allied forces, he humbly requested Leo to be given land, and for his people to be accepted as federates of the Empire. The request was granted, and the Huns remained in the Dobruja area between the Danube and the Black Sea in the eastern part of modern Roumania.[2]

The life they led there is known only through archaeology, from the evidence of saddles and rings, pots and diadems, arrows and necklaces. There were no chroniclers to tell of challenges to the Byzantine Empire, or exchanges of embassies, of military exploits, of a court life of distinction. The contrast between the eight years of Attila's rule and, first, the defeats and humiliations suffered by his sons and, later, the anonymity of their successors could hardly have been greater.

CHAPTER 24

EMPIRES DISSOLVE

Attila and the only two military leaders who defied him with any success, Aetius and Thorismund, all died within a period of about a year. Neither Aetius nor Thorismund had a peaceful end.

After Attila's withdrawal from Italy, Aetius, who had probably been fortunate in not having to engage in battle with Attila a second time, was in a position of strength. There is no evidence that he had any designs on the imperial throne for himself, but he certainly had ambitions for his family.

He had a son named Gaudentius, who, he hoped, would be allowed to marry the daughter of the Emperor Valentinian. This plan was opposed by a well-known figure in Roman society, who, although already nearing sixty, still had ambitions of his own.

His name was Petronius Maximus. He had twice been Prefect of Rome and twice Consul, and he had even had a statue erected to him in Trajan's Forum, following a petition on behalf of the Senate and people. Sidonius wrote of his 'conspicuous way of life, his banquets, his lavish expense, his retinues, his literary pursuits, his estates, his extensive patronage.'

All this evidently did not satisfy him, and he was determined to thwart Aetius. For this purpose he enlisted the help of a courtier and eunuch named Heraclius, to whom Valentinian was inclined to listen. Whether Heraclius also resented Aetius's power, or whether he merely enjoyed intrigue, is not known, but he agreed to join Petronius in his plot. Together they persuaded Valentinian that Aetius planned to assassinate him and that he would be wise to have him removed.

Aetius called on Valentinian to present him with a financial statement.

He was not of course armed. Valentinian was sitting on his throne, and without warning he drew a sword, rushed on Aetius and stabbed him to death. Soon afterwards he was reputedly told: 'You have cut off your right hand with your left. Who is now to save Italy from the Vandals?'[1] The year was 454, some twelve months after the death of Attila.

Petronius and Heraclius soon fell out, Heraclius persuading Valentinian that, having freed himself of the threat from Aetius, he would be unwise to allow Petronius to become even more powerful than he already was.

Petronius decided to act again, this time enlisting two soldiers named Optila and Thraustila, said to be barbarians, who had served under Aetius in a number of his campaigns. He persuaded them that it was their duty and in their interest to avenge Aetius's death and called their attention to one of Valentinian's habits. This was to visit the Campus Martius, where he would have a little archery practice or watch the athletes exercising.

Following Petronius's instructions, the two soldiers hid behind some laurel bushes. Then, as the Emperor passed, they rushed out and killed him with their swords. Valentinian's guards seem to have offered no defence.

Petronius became Emperor, a position which he held for seventy days, in 455. His end came as a Vandal fleet approached the Italian coast with the evident intention of attacking Rome. In the panic that ensued, Petronius's personal guard mutinied, killed him, cut his body into pieces, and threw them into the Tiber.

How Aetius, who for so long had defended the Roman Empire in the West with such skill, would have responded to the Vandal threat can only be guessed. One man who had also confronted Attila did however act. This was Pope Leo I, who interceded with the Vandals as he had done with the Huns. He could not prevent the Vandals, who were even more powerful than Alaric's army had been, from entering Rome as conquerors. But he did persuade them, as a Christian Pope addressing Christians, to cause no more damage than need be to people and buildings, churches in particular.

Thorismund reigned as Visigoth King for some two years after his father had been killed in action on the Catalaunian Fields. In 453 he was assassinated and replaced by his brother, Theodoric II, the ruler who made such an impression on Sidonius. This act of violence suggests that Thorismund had good reasons for leaving the Catalaunian Fields as precipitately as he did in order to look after his interests at home. His mild rule, which Jordanes praised so highly, was not exercised for long.

One close associate of Attila did survive him by more than twenty years: his secretary, Orestes, who had played an important part in the discovery of the plot to have Attila murdered concocted by the eunuch Chrysaphius in Constantinople. Orestes was to be a figure of significance in the final years of the Western Roman Empire.

The emperors who succeeded Petronius were of a variety of racial origins, reigned for brief periods and were, for the most part, nominees of the half-Suevian, half-Visigoth soldier and adventurer Ricimer.

Ricimer spent much of his youth at the court of Valentinian III and served in a military capacity under Aetius. He later had the rare distinction of defeating Vandal forces at sea off Corsica and on land in Sicily. The Emperor Leo I in Constantinople granted him the title of Patriarch. In this role he appointed a succession of undistinguished emperors in the West and arranged the murder of more than one of them.

Ricimer died in 472. After his death Orestes replaced him to some extent in the king-making role, albeit in a much less devious manner.

After Attila's death Orestes entered the imperial service, in which his father-in-law was already a powerful figure, and rose to command the household troops of one of Ricimer's nominees, the Emperor Anthemius. Anthemius's successor, Julius Nepos, had Orestes promoted to supreme command of the army. In this capacity he ordered him to go to Gaul. Orestes refused, secured the support of the army, and forced the Emperor to leave Italy.

Like Ricimer, Orestes did not seek the throne for himself, but in October 475 he had his son Romulus proclaimed Emperor. Romulus was only a child and became known by the derogatory diminutive name 'Augustulus'. Orestes, who had already advanced far after leaving the service of Attila, clearly planned to control the Empire through his son.

That he did not succeed was mainly because of the demands made by the many Gothic and other mercenaries who had for long been sustaining emperors and pretenders to the imperial throne. A group of them demanded territory amounting to about a third of Italy in which they could settle their followers, and over which they could exercise sovereignty. Orestes refused, and the mercenaries turned to a new leader named Odoacer.

Odoacer belonged to the Skirian tribe. His father's name was Edika and he may well have been the king who was involved in the plot to murder Attila conceived by Chrysaphius.[2] Odoacer had enlisted in the imperial army as a young man and had advanced far. When some of the mercenaries discussed plans to rebel against Orestes he felt strong enough to assure them that he would obtain what they wanted if they agreed to crown him.

The rebellion took place. Orestes fled first to Pavia, then to Piacenza, where he was captured and killed. Odoacer returned to Ravenna, one of his immediate tasks being to decide what was to be done with the youthful Emperor Romulus.

Romulus was a quiet, harmless, good-looking boy, and Odoacer, after telling him he must abdicate, awarded him a pension and allowed him to live peacefully with other members of his family. In this way in the year 476 the Roman Empire in the West formally came to an end. Odoacer did not aspire to the title of Emperor, claiming instead that of King of Italy.

The death of Attila led to the disintegration of the Hun Empire. The murder of Aetius hastened that of the Empire of Rome, for with it came the loss of the last of an invaluable species, a military commander who repeatedly triumphed over foreign enemies while remaining the Emperor's loyal servant. Visigoth rule over a large part of France did survive the death of Thorismund, but not for long.

By the end of the fifth century the Franks had become the most powerful of the peoples occupying former Roman territory in the West. Their strength was increased when their king, Clovis, effected a valuable dynastic union with a Burgundian princess in 493. He gained additional military strength when he became a Christian and was baptized, together with three thousand other Franks, by the Archbishop of Reims on

Christmas Day 496. (While still a pagan he had, like Attila nearly half a century earlier, been denied access to Paris, according to legend, by the youthful and resourceful St Geneviève.)

Eleven years after his conversion, in 507, Clovis's army inflicted a crushing defeat on that of the Visigoth king, Alaric II, near Poitiers. As a result Visigoth territory as far as the Pyrenees was added to the Frank kingdom. The Visigoths retired to Spain, and Clovis established a new capital in Paris.

The immediate beneficiaries of the end of the Roman Empire in the West were the Ostrogoths, who enjoyed a remarkable period of peace, prosperity and attainment in the first quarter of the sixth century. This occurred during the reign of a king who bore the common Gothic name Theodoric and who replaced Odoacer as the ruler of Italy.

Theodoric spent his boyhood, from the age of seven to that of seventeen, as a hostage in Constantinople. This was followed by some twenty years of campaigning as a Gothic chieftain, which culminated in the capture of Ravenna after a long blockade in 493 and the killing of Odoacer.

What followed was in extraordinary contrast with Theodoric's earlier life. For the thirty-three years of his reign there was almost uninterrupted peace. Agriculture flourished, and Italy, instead of importing corn, was able to export it. Marshes were drained, harbours built and taxes reduced. The art of the mosaic flourished, and the people once again enjoyed their circus games. The learned Boethius, from whose translations from the Greek generations of men and women were to derive most of their knowledge of science, found a patron in Theodoric.[3]

An Arian Christian himself, Theodoric was tolerant of other creeds and either persuaded or obliged Pope John I to go to Constantinople to plead for toleration of Arianism. The Pope carried out the task assigned to him in, at best, a lukewarm manner, and on his return Theodoric put him in prison, where he died. Pope John was canonized, and one ecclesiastical chronicler portrayed Theodoric as a devil who was punished for his sins by being swallowed up by a volcano.[4]

This was something of a blemish on a reputation for excellence that caused the title 'the great' to be applied to Theodoric by more than one commentator. His visible memorial is, like that of Galla Placidia, an impressive mausoleum in Ravenna. A later Goth leader, Totila, in some respects surpassed him in liberalism by freeing large numbers of slaves and distributing land to peasants.

Theodoric envisaged the creation of a league of independent kingdoms stretching from Germany to Africa under his leadership, but interests were too divergent for the kind of unity that Charlemagne later brought about to be achieved in Theodoric's time. As one modern historian has aptly put it, the Goths could do no more than hand on Roman civilization, as though in a relay race, to a Church in whose hands it would be preserved and transformed.[5]

Just as among the peoples known as barbarians there were more successful military commanders in his century than Attila, so there were more enlightened and productive rulers. Yet the name of Theodoric, like the name of Alaric, is known mainly to students of history, and that of Totila is barely recalled. It is Attila's name, the Attila of fact or the Attila of legend, which is preserved in popular knowledge.

CHAPTER 25

THE HUNS AND THEIR SUCCESSORS

As a people, the Huns survived the various disasters that followed the death of Attila, but they largely disappeared, at least in name, from the history books.

Those Huns who settled in the Volga area after their defeats, first by Gepids, and then by imperial forces, remained independent for a century or more. Numerous traces of their presence have been recorded by archaeologists.[1]

There was an attack of some consequence by Huns against Thrace during the reign of Marcian's successor, the Emperor Leo I,[2] and it was largely because of the threat the Huns posed that an additional outer wall was added to the defences of Constantinople. But it was as mercenaries, the role they had filled with such success under Aetius, that the Huns were known for the most part to historians of the sixth century. The commander who employed them to greatest advantage was Count Belisarius, the distinguished general in the service of eastern emperors, in particular Justinian.

Belisarius was a serious student of cavalry strategy and tactics. He trained his army carefully and in 530, while still in his twenties, had the distinction, rare in an imperial commander, of gaining a comprehensive victory over the Persians.

He provided his cavalry with an improved kind of saddle and steel stirrups, and trained them in how to string bows and fire arrows when their horses were at full gallop. These methods he seems to have learned from the Huns, and he insisted that all his officers must be as good horsemen and as adept with bow, lance and sword as any of their men.

The rations that Belisarius's men carried with them were also based on Hun example.[3]

The Huns who served under Belisarius came for the most part from southern Russia and were no doubt descendants of the so-called White Huns, who had diverged from the main Hun body as it advanced into western Europe. They were still nomadic in their habits, and other members of Belisarius's army were intrigued by their taste for fermented mare's milk, or *kumys*.[4]

Belisarius seems to have commanded the unswerving loyalty of the Huns, as he did that of the rest of his heterogeneous army. After his victory over the Persians he campaigned successfully against the Vandals in North Africa, and later conquered, for the Eastern Empire, most of Italy, including Ravenna. The Goths whom he defeated even wanted to proclaim him Emperor, an offer which he declined.

On a number of his campaigns Belisarius was accompanied by his wife Antonina, and it was a servant of Antonina whom Robert Graves chose as the narrator in his masterly novel *Count Belisarius*.

Hun mercenaries left evidence of their presence in a wide variety of lands. Although it is in eastern and central Europe that these Hun artefacts predominate, they are also to be found in parts of ancient Gaul and even in more remote parts of the Roman Empire.

Some of the artefacts were no doubt brought by Attila's army. Among them were the thick bronze cauldrons which, in the words of one archaeologist, extend from Asia to the Catalaunian Fields.[5] One of these, which is today in the Hungarian National Museum in Budapest, weighs sixteen kilograms and is nearly sixty centimetres in height.

Among the Hun graves in France some are clearly those of women. One in particular, in Hochfelden in Alsace, has jewellery of a kind that may well have belonged to a princess, from which it may be deduced that she was less likely to have been a camp follower in Attila's army than the wife of a military figure of consequence, possibly the commander of a garrison.[6]

Other Hun artefacts have been found in Beja in southern Portugal, in Gránada, in various parts of North Africa, and in Gloucester.[7] The North African finds suggest the presence of Hun mercenaries either in the army of the Vandals or in some Roman expeditionary force.

The history of one chance discovery in France throws a revealing light on the way in which Attila came to be regarded, even in serious scientific circles, in western Europe.

In 1969 a farmer in the Bourges area, on returning home from his fields, found a piece of lead piping in one of the tyres of his tractor. He threw it into a bin, from which his son took it. He in turn threw it into a pond, where it remained until a servant noticed a gold object protruding from it. The lead piping concealed sixteen gold coins.

All were *solidi* and all were minted in Ravenna in the reign of Valentinian III. The reverse shows the Emperor standing, with a globe in his left hand and a cross in his right. His foot is placed on a serpent with a human face.

Earlier discoveries of similar coins had led one French archaeologist, in 1914, to advance the theory that the serpent with the human face must be a representation of Attila. The *solidi* found near Bourges are among those that effectively disprove this theory, for they were minted at the time of the accession of Valentinian, that is to say some twenty years before Attila came to power.[8]

The period to which distinctively Hun artefacts can be attributed is limited in time. This is because the Huns survived, not as a people with a culture which was unmistakably their own, but through being assimilated by, and intermarrying with, other races. One people with whom their future was indissolubly linked migrated, as they had done, to the shores of the Black Sea.

They were the Bulgars, who were racially similar to the Huns and, like them, were skilled horsemen, respected warriors living largely on the spoils of war, and predominantly meat-eaters. Siberian and Iranian influences can be traced in their culture, and in their costume they differed noticeably from the Huns. Both their men and their women wore baggy trousers, the women were sometimes veiled, and men wore large turbans over shaven heads.[9]

The irruption of the Bulgars into the Lower Danube–Black Sea region brought about the end of the Huns as an independent people of military and political consequence. From the mingling of the two peoples a new power arose which dominated much of south-east Europe for centuries and offered a continual threat to the Byzantine Empire.

One of the Bulgar tribes was largely annihilated by another nomadic and warlike people, the Avars, but by the end of the sixth century a Bulgarian state was firmly established. In 626, in alliance with the Persians, the Bulgars threatened the destruction of Constantinople, a disaster that was averted only by the military skills of the Emperor Heraclius or, as was otherwise claimed, by the direct intervention of the Virgin Mary. Half a century later the military successes of the Bulgars were such that the Emperor Constantine IV agreed to pay them an annual subsidy.

There were a number of powerful Bulgar rulers or khans in the ninth and tenth centuries. One of the less successful militarily, Boris, was to be one of the most influential, for his adoption, under some duress, of the Christian Orthodox faith was followed by the general conversion of his people. Among his successors was Simeon, of whose reign in the first quarter of the tenth century Gibbon wrote: 'Bulgaria assumed a rank among the civilized powers of the earth.' Simeon himself saw Bulgaria as a second Byzantium and even adopted the title 'basileus'.[10]

Although serving to some extent as a buffer state between the Byzantine Empire and the new Slav powers that were arising to the north and east, Bulgaria, a country peopled in part at least by Huns and their descendants of mixed race, remained a power of importance until its annexation by the Turks towards the end of the fourteenth century.

After the military disasters that followed the death of Attila, many Huns left those areas that he had ruled with such effect. Others remained, but those who did were unable to resist the onslaught of the Avars, another people who were racially similar to the Huns.

The Avars, like the Huns before them, had advanced westward by conquest. After defeating the Bulgarian Utiguri tribe they were by the middle of the sixth century in control of a considerable area between the Volga and the Elbe. In 565 they formed an alliance with another warlike and migratory people, the Lombards, an alliance which, two years later, gained a decisive victory over the Gepids. The Lombards moved on to north Italy, and the Avars occupied the Danube–Tisza plain, where Attila's capital had once been.

Like the Huns, the Avars produced a military leader of rare distinction. His name, little known to posterity, was Bayan. Under his rule the

Avars became one of the most powerful peoples in Europe. Among the tributes Bayan was able to exact from the Byzantine Empire were 120,000 pieces of gold, a golden bed and an elephant. In one campaign, after ravaging the suburbs of Constantinople, he was reputed to have carried off 270,000 prisoners.

Throughout the second half of the sixth century the Avars continued to threaten the Eastern Empire. They then, like Attila before them, turned their attention to the West, ravaging parts of Germany and Italy and making more than one irruption into Frankish territory. For two and a half centuries they were in control of the Carpathian region and much else of Central Europe, assimilating Germanic and Slav peoples as well as Huns.[11] Their power was finally broken at the end of the eighth century by the forces of Charlemagne in a prolonged and bloody campaign.

Archaeologists today distinguish without great difficulty between Hun and Avar cultures. In the museum in Szeged which houses the precious Hun gold there is a considerable display of artefacts that can confidently be attributed exclusively to the Avars. But to their contemporaries the distinction between the two peoples at the height of Avar power may not have been so clear.

The eighth-century historian known as Paul the Deacon, for example, in his history of the Lombards, wrote of 'the Huns, who are also called Avars.' This was not the only occasion on which he failed to distinguish between the two peoples, yet he was recognized as an historian of such distinction that Mommsen wrote of him: 'No one repeatedly contributed so much through his writings to secure for the world the possession of Roman and Germanic tradition as did this Benedictine monk.'[12]

The Hungarian plain, where Attila had his capital and from which, archaeological evidence and tradition suggest, the Avars may also have ruled their empire, is an exceptionally difficult area to defend militarily. In consequence one migratory people after another gained control of it and from there launched attacks on more settled lands. After the power of the Avars had been destroyed the incursions of the Magyars began.

The Magyars, like their predecessors, had migrated westward, being forced to flee in large numbers across the Carpathians. They evinced skills as horsemen similar to those of the Huns and Avars and had similar dietary habits. Having established a power base in Hungary, they too carried out a succession of raids into western Europe, advancing as far as Nîmes in southern France and the Abruzzi in Italy, causing panic and destruction wherever they went.

They did however differ from Huns and Avars in two important respects. One was their introduction of a wholly different language, which belonged to the Finno-Ugrian group and which has today some resemblances to Finnish and Estonian. The other was that so far from being overcome, expelled or assimilated by some new migratory people, they remained as the dominant power in what was to become the Kingdom of Hungary.

Many of the ancestors of modern Hungarians were no doubt Avars; others were Gepids, and others were Huns. But their descendants have been wholly absorbed in the Magyar culture with one partial exception. These are people known in Hungary as the Székely, a name that has been translated into English as 'Szeklers'. Not readily distinguishable from Magyars in appearance, they number rather less than half a million and live predominantly in Transylvania.

Some ethnologists believe they may be descended from the Avars, but, according to their own traditions, their ancestors were Huns, and it is Attila who is commonly seen as the folk-hero of their past.

CHAPTER 26

NIBELUNG AND EDDA

The Attila who has emerged over the centuries through legend and the adaptation of legend is not a clear-cut figure. Nor is he a complex yet comprehensible one. He seems rather to be a number of different beings with sharply contrasting characteristics.

Legends in which Attila was the central figure began to take shape soon after his death. Jordanes, that engaging Goth writer who described himself as 'an unlearned man' before his conversion to Christianity, wove legend into recorded fact several times in his historical work. To him we owe the account of how the Huns came to the Crimea.

Huns and Goths were reputed to have lived in close proximity for a long time without knowing of each other's existence. One day a heifer belonging to the Huns was stung by a gadfly and rushed through marshy water towards the far shore. A herdsman followed the heifer and reported to the Huns what he had seen.

'The hunters', Jordanes wrote, 'followed and crossed on foot the Maeotic swamp, which they supposed was as impassable as the sea. Presently the unknown land of Scythia exposed itself. Now in my opinion the evil spirits, from whom the Huns are descended, did this from envy of the Scythians. And the Huns, who had been widely ignorant that there was another land beyond Maeotia, were now filled with admiration of the Scythian land.'

Jordanes's account of Attila's burial may be considered another of the legends. The tale was widely told also of a sword with magic powers which was thought to have disappeared from earth. A herdsman, who was tracking a wounded heifer by the drops of her blood, found the sword fixed in the ground as if it had fallen from heaven. He presented it to Attila.

Attila did indeed possess a sword, which was thought to have belonged once to Mars, and he may well have believed, as may his followers, that this sword made him almost invincible. The sword was to reappear in legend long after Attila's death.

The earliest Roman chronicler to have described the Huns was Ammianus Marcellinus, who wrote a history of the Roman Empire in thirty-one volumes, the last eighteen of which have survived. Ammianus lived in the fourth century AD. His history ends with the death in battle of the Emperor Valens in 378.

As a professional soldier he had first-hand experience of fighting against the Franks. As an historian he was highly esteemed by Gibbon, who readily acknowledged his debt to him. A later British historian of the last centuries of the Roman Empire, A. H. M. Jones, went so far as to describe Ammianus as 'a great historian, a man of penetrating intelligence and remarkable fairness.'[1]

Campaigning does, however, seem to have given Ammianus certain prejudices against barbarians, which emerged strikingly when he wrote about Huns. One statement, for example, was manifestly untrue. This was his assertion that the Huns were not 'bound by any reverence for religion or superstition.'

There is no reason to suppose that Ammianus ever encountered a Hun, and his comments on their habits were clearly based on ill-informed rumour. Among these were that the Huns' clothes were made of the skins of field-mice and that at birth their children's faces were deeply scarred by irons.

One comment by Ammianus on the lifestyle of the Huns was to be repeated by commentators through the ages. This was that 'they are so hardy that they neither require fire nor well-flavoured food, but live on the roots of such herbs as they get in the fields, or on the half-raw flesh of any animal, which they merely warm rapidly by placing it between their own thighs and the backs of their horses.'

In truth, placing raw meat below their saddles was a traditional method of protecting the backs of their horses from excessive rubbing. Raw steaks are used today for comparable purposes.

Ammianus was not a Christian. Christian commentators who followed him tended to allow any prejudices they may have had against the Huns to be exacerbated by religious differences. Bishop Zosimus, writing of events in Thrace, made the curious statement that fugitive slaves 'pretending to be Huns pillaged all the fields and took whatever they found without doors.'[2]

One Christian commentator on the Huns, who, like Ammianus, has been frequently quoted, was St Jerome. Few of those who have been canonized could have claimed even a small portion of the range of Jerome's distinctions. He translated the Bible and the theological works of Origen, learning, in order to do so, both Hebrew and Greek. Scholarship he considered both a delight and a peril, and one crisis in his life came when he heard Christ rebuking him for wanting to be more of a Ciceronian than a Christian.

He played a leading part in fostering the spirit of monasticism. Accompanied by two rich Roman women, a widow named Paula and her daughter, and a company of maidens dedicated to the celibate life, he wandered over much of Egypt and Palestine. He and his companions settled in Bethlehem, where Paula founded four monasteries, over one of which Jerome presided. There he continued his studies. Of his own dedication to the ascetic life he wrote: 'Some people may be eunuchs of necessity; I am one of free will.'

Not everyone found St Jerome an easy man to deal with. A Regius Professor of Divinity at the University of Oxford wrote of him: 'Jerome was a prickly, donnish figure of a familiar type; his immense scholarship could at times be put to the service of passionate resentments and petty jealousies. He could not endure criticism.'[3] But he was paid heed to, no matter what subject he was considering.[4]

Of the Huns, Jerome wrote: 'Speeding hither and thither on their nimble-footed horses, they were filling all the world with panic and bloodshed. They outstripped rumour in speed, and, when they came, they spared neither religion nor rank nor age, even for wailing children they had no pity.' He added, against all evidence, that 'it was generally agreed that the goal of the invaders was Jerusalem.'

In assessing the value of Jerome's comments on the Huns it may be pertinent to take account of his observations of other strange peoples.

'Why should I speak of other nations,' he wrote in one of his letters, 'when I myself, a youth on a visit to Gaul, heard that the Atticoti, a British tribe, eat human flesh and that although they find herds of swine, and droves of large and small cattle in the woods, it is their custom to cut off the buttocks of the shepherds and the breasts of their women, and to regard them as the greatest delicacies?'

'The Scots', he went on, 'have no wives of their own; as though they read Plato's Republic and took Cato for their leader, no man among them has his own wife, but like beasts they indulge their lust to their hearts' content.'[5]

Attila as a recognizable human being, rather than an obviously mythical figure, appears in a number of Germanic and Norse legends. These legends are in part based on the same characters, but whereas in the Germanic ones Attila appears as a dignified and respected figure, in the Norse he is a crude drunkard.

The Germanic legends indicate a knowledge on the part of their compilers of the true history of the Huns. This is absent from the Norse legends, in which the Hun warriors bear little relation to the people whom Attila ruled and are even described as 'long-moustached'.

One such Germanic tale is the story of Walther and Hildegund. This tells of a nation of horsemen who, advancing from their home in Hungary and driven by the will-power of their king, Attila, conquered all the peoples of Europe. 'Those who opposed Attila were overthrown by force, but to those who yielded to him the mighty king offered protection and alliance.'[6]

The numbers of the Huns could no more be counted than the sands of the shore. The peoples of other lands found that wisdom lay in not defying them, and as a result Attila acquired large quantities of gold and silver. He received too as a hostage a handsome young man of noble birth named Hagen.

The King of the Burgundians also sent an embassy to Attila, for the Huns had invaded his territory and destroyed his forces at Châlons. Attila informed the ambassadors that he was a friend of peace and only fought with those who opposed him by force. Again gifts were offered as well as a hostage in the person of Hildegund, the Burgundian King's daughter and only child.

Attila then turned his attention to the West and invaded Aquitaine. Here too the Huns triumphed, and Attila received a new hostage, a young prince named Walther. Attila gave orders for Hagen and Walther to be brought up as if they were his own sons and married Hildegund. For all this none of the three showed much gratitude.

Hagen escaped surreptitiously by night. The central figures in the story from then on are Walther and Hildegund, who fall in love and conspire to make their escape when Attila, overcome by wine, falls asleep.

The best known of all the legendary tales in which Attila features is the *Nibelungenlied*, which arose from various versions of a story developed by tale-tellers in both Germany and Scandinavia.

In an early Norse version Sigurd, the son of a northern king, is equipped with a sword of immense power and an ability to understand the language of the birds. He meets a sleeping beauty named Brunhild, but leaves her temporarily to journey to a Rhineland court.

There he forms a friendship with the three sons of the king, one of whom is named Gunnar. The three brothers arrange a match between Sigard and their sister Gudrun. In this they are helped by their mother, Queen Grimhild, who gives Sigurd a magic drink which causes him to forget Brunhild. Gunnar decides to marry Brunhild and succeeds in doing so, but only after Sigurd, who has somehow taken Gunnar's form, rides on a magic horse through the circle of flames that protects Brunhild's honour.

Not surprisingly after all this, Gudrun and Brunhild fall out, and Brunhild, maddened by jealousy, persuades one of the brothers to kill Sigurd. When this has been achieved she climbs on Sigurd's funeral pyre and kills herself with his sword.

It is at this point in the story that Attila appears under the name of Atli, King of the Huns. A marriage has been arranged between Sigurd's widow, Gudrun, and Atli, and Atli invites her brothers to his court in the belief that he will be able to seize the gold that they are known to possess. The brothers, before leaving, take the precaution of burying the gold in the Rhine.

Further slaughter follows, this time on Atli's orders, when the brothers refuse to reveal the whereabouts of the gold. The climax comes when Gudrun, in order to avenge the death of her brothers, kills first the sons she has borne Atli, and then Atli himself. After that there is little left for her to do except leap into the sea.

The authors of the versions of the *Nibelungenlied* that posterity has come to accept and respect used something of this gruesome early story, but transformed it into an epic in which tragedy is blended with chivalry and courtly behaviour.

The Siegfried who replaces Sigurd has had wise men as his tutors, and it is not Brunhild who brings about his death, but a sinister intriguer named Hagen. Siegfried behaves as a loyal ally of the Burgundians, to whose court at Worms he has been brought, and his burial is conducted according to Christian rites. Gudrun is transformed into Kriemhild, a dignified, albeit vengeful, figure.

Attila now bears the name Etzel and appears as a wise, considerate and seemingly middle-aged man. After the death of his queen, whose name was Helca, Etzel is said to have 'wooed other women', and he expresses interest when it is suggested that he should marry Siegfried's widow, Kriemhild. But he foresees a difficulty.

'Seeing that we know so much to her credit,' he says, 'we should be pleased to see her crowned in Hungary.' But he adds: 'How could this ever come about seeing that I am a heathen?'[7] Kriemhild is also aware of this objection, but is informed that Etzel was once christened, although he 'turned again'.

The negotiations for the marriage are conducted by Count Rüdiger of Pochlarn, through whose site Attila's army must have passed on its way to Germany and France. Rüdiger, like Etzel and Kriemhild, speaks throughout in a language of courtly grace.

'"The august monarch Etzel conveys to you here in Burgundy, my lady, his great and sincere affection." "Margrave Rüdiger," answered the Queen, "if you knew the sharp pains I suffer, you would not ask me to love another man." "Mighty Queen," answered Rüdiger, "your life with Etzel will be so splendid that it will give you endless delight."'

Rüdiger and the emissaries who have come from Hungary swear to serve Kriemhild loyally always, and she agrees to go to 'the Lord of the Huns'. She brings with her twelve chests of gold and a hundred high-born maidens.

The wedding festivities continue for seventeen days. 'I do not believe', the chronicler states, 'it can be said of any king that his wedding celebrations were on a vaster scale.' Etzel and Kriemhild then live together 'in great splendour'.

Hagen, the murderer of Siegfried, arrives with sixty picked warriors, but even his appearance does nothing to abate Etzel's general bonhomie. 'Nothing would give me greater pleasure in the world', he says, 'than this your coming here to visit me, you warriors.' The chronicler adds: 'They were given meat and drink in abundance and their every wish was attended to.'

Hagen and his followers thereupon start killing the members of Etzel's immediate entourage one by one. 'Etzel's men defended themselves stoutly, but the visitors traversed the King's hall from end to end, slashing with their bright swords.'

Etzel shows exemplary courage and leadership. He calls up twenty thousand Huns, but, even with these to support him, he remains remarkably reasonable and approachable. '"Tell me what you want of me," the King asked the strangers. "You hope to gain a truce? After such vast loss as you have inflicted on me that could never be."'

The killing continues. '"All the joy that was once in Hungary has vanished away," said one of the crowd.' Rüdiger is killed, and so are all the Burgundians except Gunther and Hagen. Hagen is carrying Siegfried's sword, but Kriemhild draws it from its sheath and cuts off Hagen's head. Then she in turn is killed.

'There lay the bodies of all that were doomed to die. The noble lady was hewn in pieces. Etzel began to weep and deeply lamented both kinsmen and vassals.'

A more reasonable, humble and, in the circumstances, merciful king could hardly have been portrayed. The contrast is vivid with the crude, drunken figure of Atli in the Norse *Edda*. So too is the contrast between the Kriemhild of the *Nibelungenlied* and the Norse Gudrun.

'Then Gudrun came out to meet Atli with gilded cup to render a lord his due. "You may take and eat, Sire, in your hall joyfully from Gudrun's hands young beasts gone to the shades.'

'Atli's ale-cups rang heavy with drink as in the halls together the Huns assembled their host, long-moustached men. Brisk warriors entered. With gleaming face Gudrun, daemonic woman, darted to bring drink for the warriors. She picked out morsels to eat with the ale with repulsion for the blanched faces, and then told Atli:

'"You have, giver of swords, chewed with honey your own sons' bleeding hearts. You are digesting, proud one, slaughtered human meat, eating it with ale morsels."'

Gudrun continues in this strain for a few more stanzas until Atli 'had drunk himself weary . . . He had no weapons and did not recoil from Gudrun.'[8]

This Norse portrait is certainly the basis of one of the Attila characters that posterity came to accept. Chaucer, for instance, also accords Attila a disgraceful end in a drunken sleep, writing of him dying with shame and dishonour, and drawing the conclusion that others 'sholde lyve in sobrenesse.'

The other manifestations of Attila with which readers and audiences were to become familiar derived partly from developments of the Germanic tales and partly from rediscovery of ancient texts.

CHAPTER 27

VENETIAN AND FRENCH PORTRAYALS

The *Nibelungenlied*, Richard Wagner's greatest source of inspiration, was repeatedly edited and revised. What may be regarded as the authorized version, a poem in German of 2,379 strophes, emerged from Austria, where it had been closely examined in noblemen's houses.[1] Work of fiction though it is, there is continual evidence of a basis in fact.

From the *Nibelungenlied* text we can follow without difficulty the route taken by the Burgundians and Huns who figure so prominently in the poem. It differed hardly, if at all, from that of Attila's army in 451.

Although Siegfried ventured further north, the main body of warriors advanced along the lines of the Rhine and the Danube, the two rivers which seem to flow through the text of the poem. They set out from Worms, which was generally thought to have been the Burgundian capital, although some scholars have suggested that Mainz may have been the true seat of Burgundian power.[2]

Their final destination, known as Etzelburg, was clearly Esztergom, the city situated on the Danube between Vienna and Budapest which was the ancient capital of Hungary and the birthplace of St Stephen. When Kriemhild with her followers is on her way to visit Etzel 'knights and ladies took each other by the hand and entered the broad palace, a very handsome building past whose base the Danube flowed.'

Like Etzel, Burgundian figures in the epic are also based on historical characters. There was for instance a Burgundian King Gundahar. There was also a Queen Brunichildis, the wife of the Frankish King Sigibert I, who reigned in Worms for a time. Like the Brunhild of the Norse epic she met a violent death, being tied to a wild horse and torn to pieces.[3]

Another character based on an historical original is named Dietrich de Bern. He is generally assumed to have been the Ostrogoth King Theodoric the Great, although he is stated in the poem to have taken refuge with Etzel. There may therefore be some confusion with Theodoric I of the Visigoths, who, though an enemy rather than an ally of Attila's, was at least contemporaneous with him.[4]

These are only a few of the instances of the blending of fact and fiction in the *Nibelungenlied*. Their very number suggests that the courtly medieval German epic may be nearer to presenting the truth than many of the fictional portrayals of Attila which followed. The picture it gives of Attila as a calm, reasoning and magnanimous ruler has little in common with that which came to be generally accepted in Italy and France and, subsequently, elsewhere in the Western world.

In Renaissance Venice, Attila seems to have been a fairly well-known fictional character. Some twenty editions of a work entitled *La Guerra d'Attila, Flagello di Dio (The War of Attila, Scourge of God)* were published between the first quarter of the sixteenth century and 1632. Its author, Giovanni-Maria Barbieri, drew extensively on a long poem, *Libro d'Attila*, which recounted various fabulous and chivalrous adventures. Barbieri's work is of interest, if for nothing else, for his claim that Attila was the son of a dog by the daughter of a Hungarian king noted for persecuting Christians.

A French scholar who has studied these Italian works has speculated on the reason why there was a sudden upsurge of interest in Attila in Venice, an interest which did not immediately extend to other Italian cities. Attila's invasion in 452, the destruction of Aquileia, and the way in which refugees from Huns and Lombards had helped to create the city of Venice were all possible explanations.

Another was awareness of the new threat to Venice and the Christian Church presented by the Ottoman Turks, which was thought comparable with that of Attila. In fact Venice was not to succumb to a new conqueror until the arrival of Napoleon Bonaparte.[5]

A sixteenth-century medallion gives another picture of Attila as seen by Italian eyes. In this he is portrayed with short hair, long ears, a long beard and a drooping moustache. From his head project two goats' horns. The reverse side of the medallion shows the city of Aquileia as it was assumed to have looked before its destruction, with an abundance of defensive towers.[6]

In the seventeenth century, Attila was chosen as a subject by one of the most esteemed of French dramatists. In 1647 the pupils of the Royal College in Rouen, which was run by Jesuits, staged a play entitled *L'Épée fatale ou le fleau d'Attila (The Fatal Sword or the Scourge of Attila.)* It was almost certainly seen by a former pupil of the college, Pierre Corneille, who twenty years later was to have his own play about Attila performed.

Like his far greater successor, Racine, Corneille was deeply influenced by the works of the ancient tragedians and sought to obey the rules concerning the unities of action, place and time by which they were controlled. He also admired many of the ideals of republican Rome. Not surprisingly his dramas of Medea and Cinna are among his masterpieces, those of Pompey and Andromeda being also acclaimed with enthusiasm during his lifetime.

Other historical characters, however, appealed to him too, in particular the Spanish military adventurer Rodrigo Diaz de Vivar, generally known as El Cid. Corneille's play *Le Cid* aroused more controversy than any of his others, giving rise to triumph, envy, fierce condemnation and the disapproval of Cardinal Richelieu.

It was understandable therefore both that Corneille should have chosen Attila as a dramatic subject and that, to discover what was known about him, he should have turned to the ancient authors, the Byzantine chronicler Count Marcellinus and Priscus in particular.[7]

The resulting portrait is by no means an unfair one. Corneille summed it up in a preface which he wrote to the printed edition of the play published in 1667:

'Attila's name is well known, but not everyone has an understanding of his character. He was a man of intellect rather than of action and sought to divide his enemies. He attacked defenceless peoples in order to strike terror in others, and exacted tribute through their fears. He exercised such dominion over the kings who accompanied him that, had he commanded them to commit parricide, they would not have dared to disobey him.

'It is not clear what his religion was. The title "Scourge of God", which he himself assumed, indicates that he did not believe in a plurality of deities. I would have supposed him to be an Arian, like the Ostrogoths and the Gepids in his army, but for the number of his wives, which in this play I have reduced. He certainly believed in soothsayers, and possibly they were all he did believe in.'

Corneille entrusted his play to Molière, whose company staged it on 4 March 1667 at the Petit Bourbon Théâtre. There were twenty performances, which at that time represented a modest success, but there was little critical acclaim. Corneille was generally agreed to have lost some of his powers as a dramatist by the time he wrote *Attila* and another play named *Agesilas*. Nicholas Boileau, who, partly through his own powers of perception and partly through the favour of Louis XIV, enjoyed an almost unique status and power as a critic, expressed his opinion clearly when he wrote:

> Après l'Agesilas
> Hélas!
> Mais après l'Attila
> Holà!

Corneille himself admitted to having difficulty in adapting what he knew of the historical figure of Attila to the demands of the French classical stage. In his preface he wrote: 'Attila twice demanded from the Emperor Valentinian his sister Honoria with grave threats and, while awaiting his answer, married Ildione. All historians write of her beauty but without mentioning her birth. This emboldened me to make her the sister of one of our first kings in order to oppose the rising power of France to the Empire in decline.'

Corneille went on to state that, according to Count Marcellinus, Attila was killed on his wedding night by his wife and added: 'I wanted to put the idea of killing him into her mind as an idea which did not materialize. The other reports state that he suffered from nose-bleeds, and that the fumes from the wine and the meat he had consumed blocked the passage of blood, which, after suffocating him, poured out violently through all apertures.

'I have followed them so far as the nature of his death is concerned, but I have thought it more appropriate to attribute its cause to an excess of rage than to intemperance.'

Attila, in short, could not easily be made into the central figure of a stage tragedy. He was neither a Christian nor an antique Roman, nor was he a figure from Greek mythology. He did not even espouse a cause with which the audience could sympathize. He had to die on stage, as the conventions demanded, but as death at the hand of a wife by way of avenging her family – the kind of death featured in the Norse *Edda* – did not appeal to Corneille, he could find no satisfactory outcome. Death by rage is neither more appealing nor more convincing than death by drink.

In discarding death as the outcome of a drinking bout, Corneille was defying what was already an accepted tradition, as the words of Chaucer show. But in doing so he probably showed sound historical judgement. Attila may well have drunk too much on his final wedding night, but the suggestion that he was a perpetual toper clearly runs counter to Priscus's first-hand account of his exceptionally temperate habits.

Bad Corneille, it has to be admitted, can be just as tedious as bad English Restoration drama, and *Attila* can hardly be classified as good Corneille. But it was a respectable attempt to portray in convincing fashion someone who, as Corneille pointed out in his preface, was well known by name to many who had little, if any, knowledge of his life and nature. That Attila the man and the period in which he lived interested Corneille deeply is shown by his choice, as another subject of drama, of Pulcheria, the sister of Theodosius II and wife of the Emperor Marcian.

CHAPTER 28

DRAMA AND OPERA

In the eighteenth and nineteenth centuries dramatists in more than one country chose Attila and his times as the theme of what was intended as a major work. One of them was the richly talented poet, composer and singer, as well as playwright, who took the name Metastasio.

As a small boy, Pietro Trapassi, as he was then called, the son of an Assisi grocer, attracted the attention of his future patron by reciting improvised poems in the street. By the age of twelve he had translated the *Iliad* into verse. He was only thirty-one when, in 1730, with a lengthy list of successful plays to his credit, he was appointed court poet to the theatre in Vienna, the city where he remained for the next fifty-two years.

Metastasio's plays were translated into a number of languages. One of them, entitled *Aetius*, was performed in London at the Theatre Royal, Haymarket, in 1732.

The opening lines are addressed by Aetius to Valentinian III. In the somewhat laboured translation by a certain Mr Humphreys they read:

> Conquest, my Lord, is ours; the fugitive
> And trembling Attila has left the Field
> To raging Desolation; Streams of Blood
> Have roll'd a Crimson Deluge o'er the Plain;
> The Brave, the Vile, the Victor, and the Vanquish'd,
> Were undistinguish'd in that Scene of Terror.

Metastasio portrays Honoria as being secretly in love with Aetius. ('Too well, alas, too well my Soul adores him.') But, for the rest, the drama is based roughly on the recorded accounts of the deaths of Aetius and Valentinian. The principal villain is Petronius Maximus, who is at least given the excuse for his actions that Valentinian tried to seduce his wife. Attila is little more than a barbarian king whose ambitions have fortunately been thwarted.

In Zacharias Werner's *Attila, A Tragedy*, by contrast, Attila is not only the central figure, but his opening lines leave no doubt in the audience's mind about the kind of man he is. The play was performed in London in 1832, and in the English version Attila begins by stating:

> Blood must still be shed
> As incense to the mighty God of war.
> He ne'er shall sheathe his sanguinary sword
> Whilst, from their Scythian haunts, the gallant Hun
> Can, like a torrent, swell'd by mountain floods,
> Pour forth his sons to battle.

The closing lines of this opening speech are:

> May the walls
> Of busy cities crumble into ruins,
> And havoc so distort the face of nature,
> That the Creator scarce shall know his work.
> For Attila is lord of all – but heaven.

Attila goes on to pour scorn on 'Byzantium's sons, whom lewdness has unsex'd', and announces his intentions by stating:

> I'll face their legions
> And, in the broad, unblinking eye of day,
> Strew the fair prospect with their recreant limbs
> And call the vultures to their carousal.

Much of the action revolves around the mutual antipathy between Attila and his brother Bleda. Attila addresses Bleda as 'dull driveller' and asks: 'Shall the Huns bend to such a thing as thou?' He reminds

Bleda, in case he might have forgotten, that the skulls of slaughtered captives are 'the native war-cups of the Huns.'

Ildico is already married to Attila, much to her distress. 'I am pair'd with one my heart abhors.' She and Bleda plot to kill Attila, and Attila instructs his guards to dispose of Bleda. This they evidently fail to do, even though one who serves Attila addresses him as 'Omnipotent on earth'.

In the second act the scene is the court in Constantinople, and the events that take place are based fairly accurately on the account given by Priscus until Bleda enters dressed as a Greek. 'The world's my country and revenge my god.'

In a later act Honoria comes to Attila's tent. He declares: 'We like a Christian bride.' But she is undecided. 'Sire! I would not press a marriage while the clang of angry war rings ominous around us.'

The climax comes in the fifth act as Aetius and Theodoric approach Attila's camp. It is Honoria, not Ildico, who kills Attila, an action that commands Attila's respect. 'Thy courage woos my admiration.' The closing line is given to Bleda:

'Ha! Is he dead? The tyrant dead? Ha! Ha!'

At this point the stage direction states: 'Laughs hysterically.'

Attila seems never to have served successfully as a tragic hero of straight drama. Corneille came near at moments to arousing the audience's sympathies, but elsewhere, depicted as a pitiless tyrant, Attila has little to commend him to anyone. Macbeth has a hideous record of murder and betrayal, and Lady Macbeth is the principal instigator of evil. But Macbeth at bay and Lady Macbeth destroyed by her own actions arouse, if not our sympathy, at least our pity. Attila, conceived as the enemy of the right and the good, fails even to do that. We can like and respect the Etzel of the *Nibelungenlied*, but not the Attila whom Renaissance Italy, drawing on classical sources, offered as a model for posterity to copy.

Dramatically by far the most successful portrayal of Attila is to be found in opera. This was recognized, at least in part, by those who attended a first performance at the Fenice Theatre in Venice on 17 March 1846. At the end of it they conducted the opera's composer, Giuseppe Verdi, in a torchlight procession to the hotel where he was staying. They did so partly as a tribute to Verdi's music and the opera's other attributes, but rather more as a form of political demonstration.

Verdi studied Werner's work closely, but in his own opera, with libretto by Temistocle Solera, the number of characters is greatly reduced, being no more than six. They are Attila; a Roman general named Ezio, who is clearly based on Aetius; two prominent citizens of Aquileia, Foresto, a knight sung by a tenor, and Odabella, the daughter of a nobleman sung by a soprano; a slave of Attila's called Uldino, who, in spite of bearing a name similar to that of the ancient Hun ruler, is stated to be a Breton; and Pope Leo I. The parts of Attila and the Pope are both sung by bass voices.

The prologue is set in a square in Aquileia, where the Huns are celebrating victory with praise of Attila and invocations to Wotan. Then Odabella, the heroine, leads a chorus which tells of the invincible spirit of Italian women, who fight alongside their men. This delighted the audience which, later that evening, was to stage the torchlight procession to Verdi's hotel.

Verdi, a dedicated patriot, was already in trouble with the ruling Austrian authorities. Some of his most rousing melodies had become patriotic airs, and not a little of the success of his opera *Nabucco* was attributable to its evident call for the liberation of an enslaved people.

When Ezio, still in the prologue, offers Attila the rest of the world provided he himself can retain Italy (*'Avrai tu l'universo, resti l'Italia a mi'*) and Attila scornfully refuses, the political implications are obvious. So are they in the scene in which Foresto and his followers proclaim their determination to build on their isolated lagoon the splendid city of Venice.

In the first scene in Act One, Odabella laments the killing of her father by Attila and, when reproached by Foresto for her status as Attila's captive, likens herself to Judith, who saved Israel.

The second part of the act takes place in Attila's tent, with Attila lying on a bed covered by a tiger skin. He tells his Breton slave Uldino of a dream in which an old man warned him against continuing his march on Rome. In spite of this he begins to assemble his army when voices can be heard in the distance of children and virgins, who are taking part in a procession led by an old man. The old man proves to be Pope Leo I, who repeats to Attila the very words he had already heard in his dream. This proves decisive, and Attila bows to the will of heaven.

Even this scene was accorded contemporary political significance by the audience, for there was a widespread belief among champions of Risorgimento that Italy could only recover her greatness as a nation under the guidance of a liberal Pope. In fact Pius IX was to be elected Pope shortly after the first performance of Verdi's *Attila*, though in reality he was far from the revolutionary Italian liberals had hoped for.

Act Two contains another patriotic aria, in which Aetius expresses his love of his country and readiness, if need be, to die for it. There is also a scene in which Attila nearly drinks a cup of wine, which Foresto has poisoned, is warned by Odabella against doing so, and agrees to spare Foresto's life if Odabella marries him.

In the third and final act Ezio and Foresto conspire to have Attila killed. They are joined by Odabella, who replies to Foresto's rebukes by saying her heart always belonged to him. When Attila enters to find Odabella in Foresto's arms he, all too reasonably, reproaches all three: the girl he wanted to marry, the man whose life he has spared, and the Roman general with whom he has made a truce. Nevertheless soldiers come in and seize Attila, and Odabella delivers the final blow by stabbing him in the heart.

This, at least, is a dignified death and one that arouses our sympathy with the victim, not least because in opera the music can give emotional depth even to melodramatic happenings.

The success of the first performance in the Fenice theatre was followed by further triumphs in a number of other cities, including Ferrara, Vicenza, Trieste and, spectacularly, Milan, the centre of Austrian rule in Italy.[1] To some it seemed a belated revenge for what had happened in Aquileia fourteen hundred years earlier.

Eleven years after the first performance of Verdi's *Attila* another musical work of distinction on a similar theme was publicly heard for the first time. This was *Die Hunnenschlacht (The Battle of the Huns)* by Ferenc, or Franz, Liszt, performed in Weimar in 1857.

Liszt was inspired by a fresco by Wilhelm von Karlsbach which depicted Attila and Theodoric at the battle of the Catalaunian Fields.

In a letter describing his intentions Liszt wrote of the need for 'plenty of brass'.[2] It is not difficult, on hearing the work, to imagine the clash of arms, both between living warriors, and between the ghosts who, according to legend, continued the fight on the Catalaunian Fields. The section devoted to the ride of the Huns is particularly evocative.

As theme music for a film on Attila and the Huns it could hardly be bettered. To Liszt the battle and all that led to it represented primarily a triumph of Christianity, a triumph he tried most evidently to convey in an organ passage on the theme of *crux fidelis*.

CHAPTER 29

'THE HUN IS AT THE GATE'

Denigration of the Huns in general and of Attila in particular reached new depths in the late nineteenth and early twentieth centuries as a consequence of European wars. This process began in 1870, when German armies advanced through eastern France. The shock and horror they aroused caused the historically minded to look for a precedent in Attila's invasion in 451, and from this it was only a small step to equating fifth-century Huns with nineteenth-century Prussians.

In October 1870 the Baron de Tocqueville published in a number of newspapers in the Oise Department a pronouncement that read: 'Faced by the invasion of German hordes we should, both from duty and self-interest, turn to the annals of history to discover how in other grave situations in the past our nation was delivered from its oppressors.

'In the year 451 Attila, whom posterity has named the Scourge of God, descended on Europe at the head of his barbarian hordes numbering 500,000 warriors. "To the impetuosity of the Tartar," a historian states, "he united the dissimulation which keeps anger in check and the patience which awaits the suitable occasion." (Does one not find in this the portrait of King William and his Chancellor?)

'Nothing could resist the impetuous fury of this barbarian. "His approach," another narrator states, "struck terror into the people of Paris, who hastily abandoned their homes, until a young girl, inspired by God, the virgin of Nanterre . . ."'

The story of how St Geneviève saved Paris follows, and the conclusion implicit in de Tocqueville's pronouncement is that for France, which had been corrupted by the Second Empire, to defeat Prussia it would be necessary to return to the ways prescribed by the Church since the day Clovis was baptized.

During the war the newspaper *Echo de Paris* commented on reports of the bombardment of Reims cathedral: 'The civilized world will respond once again with a cry of horror to the savage barbarism of the Huns of the twentieth century.' Immediately after the war a writer named Layaume dedicated a book to the youth of France with the title 'Germany to the Stake! Shame and Crimes of Prussia from Attila to the Present Times!'[1]

In internal political debates the adherents of clerical parties likened the insurrectionaries of the Commune to Attila's hordes, and a pamphlet addressed to 'the Christian women of France' in 1882 attacked those politicians who had 'no doubt forgotten that it was God, whom they banished from schools, who saved Paris in 451 from invasion by people from the north.'

In 1896 a committee formed to organize the celebrations of the four hundredth anniversary of the baptism of Clovis, while calling attention to the threat of anarchy and impiety, expressed its confidence in the God who 'saved Paris from the armies of Attila by confronting the barbarian with St Geneviève', and the God who 'raised Joan of Arc to drive the English from our country which they had invaded for over a hundred years.'

When war between France and Germany broke out again in 1914 the spirit of St Geneviève was invoked with even greater frequency. Analogies were drawn between the battle of the Marne and that of the Catalaunian Fields, and satisfaction could be felt that, as in St Geneviève's time, the enemy was prevented from occupying Paris.

The identification of Huns with Germans was now commonplace, as was acceptance of the kind of sentiment expressed in a speech at an award-giving ceremony in 1916.

'Have they not appeared in those regions to the east, terrorizing populations, making appalling requisitions, taking hostages, shooting peaceful citizens after setting fire to their homes before their own eyes, torturing the old, massacring children, laughing at their tears, insulting their grief, strutting everywhere as masters of torture, pillage, fire and murder? Have they not been seen to conduct themselves as barbarians and shown themselves proud to recall Attila?"[2]

As allies of the French in World War I the British readily accepted the identification of modern Germans with ancient Huns in spite of its ethnological absurdity. The Huns had played no part in British history, but they could easily be adopted as a hate-symbol, and in the English language the word 'Hun' can be pronounced with peculiar venom.

The direction of hatred towards the new Huns certainly had an impact on the kind of people who conceived it to be a patriotic duty to destroy their dachshunds because of their German origin. Whether it had much effect on the outcome of trench warfare is more questionable. Yet even a poet as richly gifted as Kipling could descend in 1914 to writing such lines as:

> For all we have and are,
> For all our children's fate
> Stand up and take the war.
> The Hun is at the gate!

In World War II attempts were made in certain military quarters to revive the use of the word 'Hun' in order to increase the military ardour of the troops, but they had little effect. The British soldiery in general continued to refer to Germans by the almost affectionate term 'Jerry'.

Although the word 'Hun' was readily used in Britain by people who knew nothing of its proper application, references to Attila himself were much rarer. Indeed, although his name is familiar to them, the British have through the centuries contributed little to the literature concerning Attila, certainly in comparison with what emerged from the countries that his armies invaded. British scholarly works on Attila are neither numerous nor of great originality, and the same is true of works of imagination. The distinguished novelist, composer and philologue Anthony Burgess did attempt to portray Attila in fiction, but hardly in a manner worthy of his talents.

In the United States, by contrast, the life of Attila and the history of the Huns have given rise to work of greater interest.

Early in January 1960 an elderly professor named Otto Maenchen-

Helfen walked into the offices of the University of California Press, bringing with him a typescript. It was the product of a lifetime study of the Huns. A few weeks later, on 29 January, Maenchen-Helfen died. His typescript was thought at first to be a complete work, but from discussions with his widow it was learned that a mass of notes still remained to be transcribed into book form.

The eventual product issued by the University of California Press, Maenchen-Helfen's *The World of the Huns*, is a rich and diverse work. It lacks some of the precision and authority of the best modern Hungarian work on the subject, particularly that of Professor István Bóna, but it served to show how much remained, at the time of its publication, to be discovered about the Huns and the world they lived in.

It was, understandably, through films that Attila and the Huns became known to the American public generally. The earliest films on the subject of Attila were made in Italy and Germany. *Attila, Flagello di Dio*, was first shown in Italian cinemas in 1917, and in the 1920s Fritz Lang, in more than one film based on stories from the *Nibelungenlied*, showed how a mass of Hun riders, with Attila at their head, provided a ready-made subject for the film spectacular.

Lang was not the only director to arrive in Hollywood as a refugee in the 1930s and to choose Attila as a subject for a film. But whoever the director might be, the treatment of the Huns varied little. They were there to serve as horsemen en masse, fighting and being fought against, and in this respect they differed little from Red Indians. Lang indeed had to defend himself against charges of derogatory treatment of primitive peoples and, in doing so, wrote that his aim was to 'oppose the hordes of savage, Asiatic Huns to the stylized, slightly degenerate, over-civilized world of the Kings of Burgundy.'[3]

The medium could vary from propagandist tract to epic film, but in western and northern Europe and in the United States the Huns continued through the centuries to be seen in much the same light, and the epithet repeatedly applied to them is 'cruel'.

The question that remains to be answered is: can the charge of cruelty be justified? Any people whose economy is largely based on plunder and warfare must kill and loot, and for that very reason is likely to be regarded with trepidation and distaste by others. Such was the fate of the Huns, and the charge of cruelty against them was for that very reason advanced. But there were other nomadic and semi-nomadic peoples who based their economies on the same principles, and there is no serious evidence to suggest that the Huns were in any way crueller than, for example, Avars, Bulgars or Magyars when they first appeared in central Europe.

Attila himself was a military leader and responsible, as such, for the destruction of cities, Nish, Metz and Aquileia among them. For this he was forgiven neither by his contemporaries nor by posterity. Yet it is difficult to regard his actions as any more reprehensible or wanton than the punitive elimination under the Roman Empire of the cities of Corinth and Carthage or, indeed, the twentieth-century destruction of Dresden and Hiroshima. And less of a question mark would seem to hang over the strategic advantages of the actions Attila took.

Nothing that is known of Attila suggests that, other than as a military commander, he was in any way cruel. Indeed, in the one clearly documented episode in his life he showed exemplary clemency in his treatment of those who planned to assassinate him. Yet the word 'cruel' has continued to be almost synonymous with his name except in one country. That country is Hungary.

CHAPTER 30

THE HUNGARIAN TRADITION

A legend familiar to many Hungarians tells of the fate of Attila's sons. After Attila's death the sons scatter in different directions, and one of them, on being attacked by his enemies, looks up into the sky by night and sees there a host of galloping Hun warriors led by Attila's favourite, Ernak.

In some of the many versions of the legend the favourite son is given the name Csaba and is said to be Attila's son by Honoria. Attila himself is sometimes reputed to have lived to the age of a hundred and fifty and to have reigned for a hundred years.

The moral to be drawn from all the variations of the story is that, whenever Hungarians are attacked by their enemies, they need only look up to the Milky Way to see the warriors who will come to the nation's rescue. The legends also show how Attila became and remains a folk-hero and ancestral figure in the Hungarian oral tradition.

The Magyars readily accepted Attila in this role. Their illustrious chief Prince Árpad, who led his followers – men, women and children – across the Carpathians towards the end of the ninth century, and in 907 established their right to their new land by his victory near Bratislava, was said to have regarded himself as a direct descendant of Attila. Attila in turn was believed to be descended from the god Magog.[1]

Árpad, according to Hungarian tradition, considered it his birthright to occupy territory once ruled by Attila. He also attributed to Attila the building of a splendid city, which he found when he came to Hungary. The city was presumably Aquincum, for whose construction the Romans were mainly responsible.

Manuscript Hungarian accounts of Attila and his times date from the eleventh century. From them it becomes clear that Huns and Hungarians were then regarded as being one nation. In the same century the Attila cult was approved and adopted by the Hungarian royal family, who were said to possess Attila's sword on its reappearance after six centuries. One Hungarian queen, when in difficulties, had the sword smuggled to her son to enable him to gain the throne. More than one pretender, seeking to obtain the sword, died a violent death.

In the thirteenth century a history of Hungary was written by a priest, Simon Kézai, who had been chaplain to King Ladislaus IV. Ladislaus was a notoriously profligate figure, against whom Pope Nicholas IV preached a crusade, and who left no legitimate heir. Monarchy and nobility were battling for power, and Kézai declared that the nobility were the true representatives of the country. In his treatment of the Hungarian past he made it clear that the ideal figure, in his judgement, was not King Stephen, who at the end of the first millennium had been crowned by the Pope and who was subsequently canonized, but Attila, the Scourge of God.

One of the greatest treasures in the Hungarian National Library in Budapest is the beautifully illuminated *Picture Chronicle*, which was compiled between 1358 and 1370 by a priest named Márk Kálti, who had made a thorough study of earlier chronicles. One of the legends he relates tells how Árpad bought the land of Hungary from a Moravian prince in exchange for a white horse. Kálti's main theme is that a God-fearing ruler will always make his kingdom prosper, and he believes this to be shown by the history of Hungary's kings. He emphasizes strongly the continuity of the succession from Attila through Árpad to his own time, when the rulers were from the House of Anjou.

There was a renewed flowering of the Attila cult in the fifteenth century, most noticeably in the reign of Hungary's distinguished King Matthias Corvinus, who reigned from 1458 to 1490. This was an age of intellectual and artistic enlightenment as well as of military expansion.

Matthias was crowned King of Bohemia and annexed large areas of what are today Austria, Slovakia and Poland. He established his capital in Vienna, and there and in his palaces in Buda and Višegrad he entertained poets and scholars. Libraries were founded and churches built, and Matthias himself was said to spend half the night reading.

In this new society Attila was acclaimed as both warrior and enlightened ruler. Historians even attributed to him long speeches delivered in faultless classical Latin. Already by then Hungarians interested in antiquity tended to think of themselves as descendants of Attila rather than of Árpad.

A Hungarian work published in 1488 entitled *Chronica Hungaroruma* gives an illuminating explanation of how Attila came to be known as the Scourge of God. According to this, when Attila's army was on its way from Orléans to the Catalaunian Fields, it captured a hermit, who was said to have the power of prophecy. Attila therefore asked him to tell him something of his own fate.

'"Great King," the hermit said, "are you asking an ignorant man to express the will of God? What talent do you see in me, the lowest of the low? God Almighty, who rules over the whole earth, recently put into your hands his punitive sword. You are now the Scourge of God, and through your power he wants to punish all those who have left the path of righteousness."'

Then came the warnings, similar in content to those recorded by Jordanes, but different in emphasis.

'God,' the hermit says, 'will take back his sword whenever he chooses and can give it to another, so that you should know that to conquer in war is not decided by man, but rests in the power of God. This time you will submit to Roman might in battle, but the sword will not yet fall out of your hand, nor will your dominion cease.'

Hungarian tradition attributes to Attila and his army a number of creative acts during their campaigns in 451 and 452. These contrast strikingly with the destruction so readily commented on by western European historians. In Trier, the splendid city known as Roma Secunda or Roma Transalpina, which the Franks had sacked more than once before the time of Attila's invasion, Attila was credited with building a triumphal arch.

Near Douai in northern France, the city later to be frequented by English Roman Catholics, where Philip II of Spain founded a university and exiled English scholars held professorial chairs, Attila's son, Ernak, was supposed to have built a fortification. How he reached Douai from the Danube was not explained. In Udine, which is not far from Aquileia, a hill was said to have been constructed out of earth carried in the hands of Attila's soldiers, and the very name of the city was thought to derive from that of Attila's forebear, Uldin.

In times of doubt and repression as well as in those of triumph the spirit of Attila was evoked in order to inspire Hungarians. In the poetry of the 1670s, for instance, during the later stages of the struggle against the Turks, the shining examples of the ancient Scythians, of Attila and of Matthias Corvinus are contrasted with the bleakness of the contemporary scene.

Indeed, through all ages of Hungarian history Attila has been regarded with veneration, and his standing today is as high as it ever was. In modern Hungary Attila is a common Christian name. One of the principal streets in Budapest is called Attila Utca. The reconstructed battlements of Budapest's ancient castle are said to resemble Attila's tents.

A modern Hungarian writer has expressed the opinion that Attila's aim was to create and stabilize an empire in which 'each nationality could have preserved its own traditions, its own culture. They could all have developed in a dynamic network of economic and cultural relations.' This, she considered, 'was Attila's dream that never became a reality because of the King's unexpected and early death.'[2]

In 1993 an important event in the cultural life of Budapest was the staging of the rock opera *Attila*, which succeeded another patriotic work in the same genre and by the same composer, Levente Szörényi, entitled *Stephen the King*.

In commenting on a collection of Hungarian legends, another Hungarian writer stated that Attila does not need to be excused, he needs only to be understood. He added that probably only a Hungarian could do him full justice. He may be right, but I would like to think not.

For more than fifteen hundred years the contrast between the western European and the Hungarian attitudes towards Attila has been sustained. Indeed, it seems almost as if the battle of the Catalaunian Fields is still being fought in the spirit. In the view of the West, Attila remains the aggressor, the destroyer, the barbarian. In the German tradition he is a somewhat neutral figure. In Hungary he is the enlightened ruler, the national hero.

Hitherto little compromise between these judgements has been found. A gesture of reconciliation may, however, possibly be sensed in the action of a firm of Dutch bulb growers. Having developed a new strain of tulip, they decided to call it 'Attila'. The new bulb was first marketed in 1945.

NOTES

1 A Much-Maligned People

1. Priscus of Panium.

2 The Huns Move West

1. Edward Gibbon, *The Decline and Fall of the Roman Empire.*
2. László Gyula, *The Art of Migration Period.*
3. Fergus Millar, *The Roman Empire and Its Neighbours.*
4. Talk with Colonel Laszlo Korsos, Director of the Hungarian Military Museum, Budapest.
5. Cambridge Medieval History.
6. S. Bökönji, *History of Domestic Mammals in Central and Eastern Europe.*
7. Gyula Németh, *Attila es Hunjai.*
8. István Bóna, *Das Hunnenreich.*
9. Talk with Professor Bökönyi.
10. Millar, op. cit.
11. Talk with Colonel Korsos.

3 Tribal Warfare

1. Bóna, op. cit.
2. Németh, op. cit.
3. István Bóna, *A l'aube du moyen age.*
4. *Germanen, Hunnen and Awaren.* Catalogue of the German National Museum, Nuremberg.

4 The Magnet of Empire

1. Agathias of Byzantium.
2. The Acts of the Apostles, Chapter 22.
3. A. H. M. Jones, *The Later Roman Empire 284–602.*
4. J. B. Bury, *History of the Later Roman Empire.*

5. E. A. Thompson, *A History of Attila and the Huns*.
6. Count Zosimus, *History*.

5 Attila Becomes King of the Huns

1. Bóna, *Das Hunnenreich*.
2. Thompson, op. cit.
3. Bóna, *Das Hunnenreich*.
4. Priscus.
5. J. Otto Maenchen-Helfen, *The World of the Huns*.
6. Gibbon, op. cit. Bóna, *Das Hunnenreich*.
7. Priscus.

6 Attila's Kingdom

1. Maenchen-Helfen, op. cit.
2. Bóna, *Das Hunnenreich*.
3. Priscus.
4. Ibid.
5. Maenchen-Helfen, op. cit.
6. Denis Sinor, entry on 'Hun religion' in *Macmillan's Encyclopedia of Religion*.
7. Béla Kézdy, *Certain Totemistic Elements in Hungarian Armory*. Attila's Armorial.
8. Henry Chadwick, *The Early Church*.
9. Ibid.
10. R. H. C. Davis, *A History of Medieval Europe*.
11. *Germanen, Hunnen und Awaren*.
12. Talks with Dr Otto Trogmayer, Director of Szeged Museum.

7 The Threat to Constantinople

1. Bóna, *Das Hunnenreich*.
2. Thompson, op. cit.
3. Ibid.
4. Maenchen-Helfen, op. cit.
5. Gibbon, op. cit.

8 The City Constantine Built

1. C. W. C. Oman, *The Byzantine Empire*.
2. John Ball, *A Description of the City of Constantinople*.
3. Bury, op. cit.
4. Michael Grant, *The Climax of Rome*.
5. Ibid.
6. Jones, op. cit.

9 The Court of Theodosius II

1. St Gregory Nazianzen, quoted by John Julius Norwich, *Byzantium. The Early Centuries*.
2. Norwich, op. cit.
3. Bury, op. cit.
4. Jones, op. cit.
5. Priscus.
6. Bury, op. cit., and Ball, op. cit.

10 A Plot to Murder Attila

11 The Murder Plot Discovered

The primary source throughout is Priscus.

12 The Weakness of the West

1. Priscus.
2. Thompson, op. cit.
3. Gibbon, op. cit.
4. Ibid.

13 The Empress in Ravenna

1. St Augustine, *The City of God*.
2. Antonio Paolucci, *Ravenna*.
3. Sidonius Apollinaris, quoted in Bury, op. cit.

4. Gibbon, op. cit.
5. Stewart Irvin Oost, *Galla Placidia Augusta*.

14 The Revival of the Western Empire

1. Etienne Paillard, *Essai sur l'ancien itinéraire de Metz à Orléans et la localisation de la défaite d'Attila en 451*.
2. Gregory of Tours, *History of the Franks*.
3. Philip Dixon, *Barbarian Europe*.
4. Gibbon, op. cit.
5. Robert Latouche, *Caesar to Charlemagne*.
6. The *Nibelungenlied* (translated by A. T. Hatto).

15 Proposal of Marriage

1. Bóna, *Das Hunnenreich*.
2. Bury, op. cit.
3. Oost, op. cit.
4. Bóna, *Das Hunnenreich*.
5. Map in Hungarian National Museum, Budapest.
6. Heinz Firmenich, *Koln–St Ursula*.
7. Information from Dr Böhringer, Director, Historiosches Archiv, Cologne.
8. Talk with Dr Ernst Englisch in Krems.
9. Gesta Trevivorum, quoted by Maenchen-Helfen, op. cit.

16 Invasion of France

1. Paillard, op. cit.
2. Latouche, op. cit.
3. Christian Amalvi, *Les influences danubiennes dans l'ouest de l'Europe au V siècle*.*
4. André Marsat, *La Campagne des Gaules dans l'hagiographie*.*

17 Battle Is Joined

1. Latouche, op. cit.
2. Paillard, op. cit.
3. Bóna, *Das Hunnenreich*.

18 The Catalaunian Fields

1. Edward S. Creasy, *The Fifteen Decisive Battles of the World*.
2. Maenchen-Helfen, op. cit.
3. Creasy, op. cit.
4. Ibid.
5. Bóna, *Das Hunnenreich*.
6. Viscount D'Abernon, *The Eighteenth Decisive Battle of the World*.
7. Maenchen-Helfen, op. cit.

19 Invasion of Italy

1. Bóna, *Das Hunnenreich*.
2. Talk with Colonel Korsos.
3. Ibid.
4. Michael Carver, *Harding of Petherton*.
5. Talk with Colonel Korsos.
6. Alta Macadam, *Northern Italy*.

20 The Cities of Lombardy Fall

1. Gibbon, op. cit.
2. *Encyclopaedia Britannica*, entry on Verona.
3. Jones, op. cit.
4. Bury, op. cit.
5. Gibbon, op. cit.

21 Attila and the Pope

1. Trevor Jalland, *The Life and Times of Leo the Great*.
2. Chadwick, op. cit.
3. Pierre Grimal, entry in *Larousse World Mythology*.
4. Jalland, op. cit.
5. Claude Moatti, *The Search for Ancient Rome*.
6. Bury, op. cit.
7. Maenchen-Helfen, op. cit.
8. Gibbon, op. cit.
9. Jordanes.

22   *The Wedding Night and After*

1. Thompson, op. cit.
2. Ibid.
3. Bóna, *Das Hunnenreich*.
4. Ibid.
5. Thompson, op. cit.
6. Bóna and Dr Ottó Trogmayer, Director of the Mora Ferenc Museum, Szeged.
7. Talk with Dr Ottó Trogmayer.

23 *The Sons of Attila*

1. Bóna, *A l'aube du moyen age*.
2. Bóna, *Das Hunnenreich*.

24 *Empires Dissolve*

1. Bury, op. cit.
2. Norwich, op. cit.
3. Robert S. Lopez, *The Birth of Europe*.
4. Ibid.
5. Robert Fossier, *Cambridge Illustrated History of the Middle Ages*.

25 *The Huns and Their Successors*

1. Bóna, *Das Hunnenreich*.
2. Benedictus Niese, *Grundriss der römischen Geschichte*.
3. Robert Graves, *Count Belisarius*.
4. Ibid.
5. Katalin Biro-Sey, *La découverte monétaire de Szikancs (Hongrie)*.*
6. Michel Kazanski, *Les influences danubiennes en Gaulle à la fin du IV et au V siècles*.*
7. Ibid.
8. Jean Lafaurie, *451: La monnaie de la victoire*.*

9.   *Encyclopaedia Britannica*, entry on Bulgaria.
10. Romilly Jenkins, *Byzantium: The Imperial Centuries*.
11. Ibid.
12. Gyula, op. cit.

26 Nibelung and Edda

1.   Jones, op. cit.
2.   Zosimus, *History*.
3.   St Jerome, *Letters*.
4.   Chadwick, op. cit.
5.   St Jerome, op. cit.
6.   *Deutsche Heldensagen*, ed. Edmund Mundrak.
7.   The *Nibelungenlied*.
8.   *The Poetic Edda* (translated by Ursula Dronke).

27 Venetian and French Portrayals

1.   Jean-Marie Levesque, *La Chanson des Nibelungen*.*
2.   Oltfried Ehrismann, *Nibelungenlied–Epoche–Werk–Wirkung*.
3.   Ibid.
4.   Levesque, op. cit.
5.   Alain R. Girard, *Un Attila de papier*.*
6.   Jacqueline Pilier-Lemiere, *Les 'Attila' des humanistes*.*
7.   Jacqueline Delaporte-Arnal, *Attila de Pierre Corneille*.*

28 Drama and Opera

1.   Jean-Jacques Bertaux, *Le mythe d'Attila, Verdi et le risorgimento*.*
2.   Performance at Royal Albert Hall, London, on 12 August 1991. Notes.

29 'The Hun Is at the Gate'

1.   Christian Amalvi, *Le mythe d'Attila et des Huns dans la société française 1830–1920*.*
2.   Ibid.
3.   Jean-Marie Levesque, *Attila au XX siècle*.*

30 The Hungarian Tradition

1. Gyula Németh, *Attila es Hunjai*.
2. Júlia Szekrényesy.

* Paper submitted to the conference and exhibition organized by the French Ministry of Culture at the Normandy Museum, Caen, in 1990.

SELECT BIBLIOGRAPHY

I have listed below only those works on which I have drawn to advantage in writing this book:

ALDUC-LE BAGOUSSE, ARMELLE, *La présence d'étrangers dans la plaine de Caen (IVe et Ve siècles)**

AMALVI, CHRISTIAN, *Le mythe d'Attila et des Huns dans la société française 1830–1920**

AMMIANUS MARCELLINUS, *History* (trans. C. D. Yonge, Bohn, London, 1862)

AUGUSTINE, ST, *The City of God*

BALL, JOHN, *A Description of the City of Constantinople* (London, 1729)

BAYNES, N. H., and MOSS, H. ST. L. B., *Byzantium. An Introduction to East Roman Civilization* (Clarendon Press, 1948)

BERTAUX, JEAN-JACQUES, *Le mythe d'Attila, Verdi et le risorgimento**

BIRO-SEY, KATALIN, *Les Huns en Europe: Un bref aperçu**

BÖKÖNYI, S., *History of Domestic Mammals in Central and Eastern Europe* (Akademiai Kiado, Budapest, 1974)

BÓNA, ISTVÁN, *Das Hunnenreich* (Corvina, Budapest, 1992)

——, *A l'aube du moyen âge* (Corvina, Budapest)

BURY, J. B., *History of the Later Roman Empire* (Macmillan, 1923)

CHADWICK, HENRY, *The Early Church* (Hodder & Stoughton, 1968)

CHOSSENOT, MICHEL, *L'Appellation du camp d'Attila à la Cheppe (Marne)* (Société d'Agriculture, Commerce, Sciences et Arts du Département de la Marne, Châlons-sur-Marne, 1967)

CREASY, SIR EDWARD S., *The Fifteen Decisive Battles of the World*

CSALLÁNY, DEZSÖ, *Archaeologische Denkmäler der Gepiden in Mitteldonaubecken (454–568)* (Hungarian Academy of Science, Budapest, 1961)

D'ABERNON, VISCOUNT, *The Eighteenth Decisive Battle of the World* (Hodder & Stoughton, 1931)

DANIÉLOU, JEAN, and MARROU, HENRI, *The First Six Hundred Years* (trans. Vincent Cronin, Darton, Longman & Todd, 1964)

DAVIS, R. H. C., *A History of Medieval Europe* (Longman, 1970)

DELAPORTE-ARNAL, JACQUELINE, *Attila de Pierre Corneille**

DIXON, PHILIP, *Barbarian Europe* (Elsevier-Phaidon)

——, *Edda* (trans. Ursula Dronke, Oxford University Press, 1969)

EHRISMANN, OTFRIED, *Nibelungenlied–Epoche–Werk–Wirkung* (Beck, Munich)

EUNAPIUS, *The Lives of the Sophists* (trans. Wilmer Cave Wright, Putnam, 1922)

FOSSIER, ROBERT, *Cambridge Illustrated History of the Middle Ages* (Guild Publishing, 1989)

Germanen, Hunnen und Awaren. Catalogue of Exhibition in Germanisches Nationalmuseum, Nürnberg (Verlag des Germanischen Nationalmuseum, 1988)

GIBBON, EDWARD, *The Decline and Fall of the Roman Empire*

GIRARD, ALAIN R., *Un Attila de papier**

GORDON, C. D., *The Age of Attila* (Ann Harbor, 1966)

GRANT, MICHAEL, *The Climax of Rome* (Weidenfeld & Nicolson, 1968)

GRAVES, ROBERT, *Count Belisarius* (Cassell, 1938)

GREGORY OF TOURS, *Histoire des Francs* (Didier, Paris, 1874)

GRIMAL, PIERRE, *World Mythology* (Larousse, Hamlyn, 1965)

GROUSSET, *L'Empire des steppes* (Payet, Paris, 1939)

GWATKIN, H. M., and WHITNEY, J. P., *Cambridge Medieval History* (Cambridge University Press, 1967)

GYÚLA, LÁSZLÓ, *The Art of Migration Period* (Corvina, Budapest)

JALLAND, TREVOR, *The Life and Times of St Leo the Great* (Macmillan, New York, 1941)

JENKINS, R., *Byzantium: The Imperial Centuries* (Weidenfeld & Nicolson, 1966)

——, *Byzantium: The Later Years*

JEROME, ST, *Letters and Select Works* (Parker, Oxford, 1893)

JONES, A. H. M., *The Later Roman Empire 284–602* (Blackwell, 1964)

JORDANES, *The Gothic History* (trans. Charles Christopher Mierow, Princeton University Press, 1915)

KAZANSKI, *Les influences danubiennes en Gaulle**

KÉZDY, BÉLA, *Certain Totemistic Elements in Hungarian Armory. Attila's Armorial* (Magyar Sociedad Científica Cultural, Buenos Aires, 1963)

LAFAURIE, JEAN, *451: La monnaie de la victoire**

LATOUCHE, ROBERT, *Caesar to Charlemagne* (Barnes & Noble, 1968)

LEIGH-FERMOR, PATRICK, *A Time of Gifts* (Murray, 1977)

LEVESQUE, JEAN-MARIE, *La chanson des Nibelungen**

——, *Attila au XXe siècle**

LOPEZ, ROBERT S., *The Birth of Europe* (Phoenix House, 1969)

MACARTNEY, C. D., *Hungary. A Short History* (Edinburgh University Press, 1962)

MAENCHEN-HELFEN, J. OTTO, *The World of the Huns* (University of California Press, 1973)

MARIN, JEAN-YVES, *La campagne des Gaulles dans l'hagiographie**

——, *Les Huns sortent de l'histoire**

SELECT BIBLIOGRAPHY

MCEVEDY, COLIN, *The Penguin Atlas of Medieval History* (Penguin)

METASTASIO, *Aetius* (T. Wood, 1732)

MILLAR, FERGUS, *The Roman Empire and Its Neighbours* (Weidenfeld & Nicolson, 1967)

MUNDRAK, EDMUND (ed), *Deutsche Heldensagen* (Ennslin-Laiblin, Reutlingen)

——, *Nibelungenlied* (trans. A. T. Hatto, 1965)

NIESE, BENEDICTUS, *Grundriss der römischen Geschichte* (Bech, 1923)

NORWICH, JOHN JULIUS, *Byzantium. The Early Centuries* (Viking, 1988)

OOST, STUART IRVIN, *Galla Placidia Augusta* (University of Chicago Press, 1968)

PAILLARD, ETIENNE, *Essai sur l'ancien itinéraire de Metz à Orléans et la localisation de la défaite d'Attila en 451* (Société d'Agriculture, Commerce, Sciences et Arts du Département de la Marne, Châlons-sur-Marne, 1967)

PAOLUCCI, ANTONIO, *Ravenna* (Edizioni Salva, Ravenna, 1971)

PAUL, DEACON OF AQUILEIA, *History of the Langobards* (trans. W. D. Foulkes, University of Pennsylvania Press, 1907)

PILIER-LEMIERE, JACQUELINE, *Les 'Attila' des humanistes**

PRISCUS OF PANIUM, *History*

PROCOPIUS, *History of the Wars*

REY-DELQUE, MONIQUE, *Attila aux portes de Rome selon Raphael**

SINOR, DENIS, *Hun Religion* (Macmillan's Encyclopedia of Religion)

SOMMERAND, LOUIS DE, *Honoria. L'amoureuse d'Attila* (Perrin, Paris, 1934)

THOMPSON, E.A., *A History of Attila and the Huns* (Oxford University Press, 1948)

TODD, MALCOLM, *Everyday Life of the Barbarians, Goths, Franks and Vandals* (Batsford, 1972)

TREVOR-ROPER, HUGH, *The Rise of Christian Europe* (Thames & Hudson, 1965)

VALLET, FRANÇOISE, *La fin de la mode danubienne**

——, *La tombe princière d'Hochfelden* (Bas Rhin)*

WERNER, ZACHARIAS, *Attila, A Tragedy* (T. W. Boone, 1832)

ZANNONI, GUGLIELMO, *Leone i Magno* (Liber Pontificalis, 1955)

ZOSIMUS, COUNT, *History*

* Paper submitted to the conference and exhibition organized by the French Ministry of Culture at the Normandy Museum, Caen, in 1990.

INDEX